The majority of mot[...] decisions about returning tc [...] e care of others.

Julia Brannen an[...] first-time mothers working in [...] talked to them before the bir[...] months afterwards when the [...] ed their decisions about empl[...] arrangements.

NEW MOTHERS [...] features the first-hand accounts of these women as they discuss the issues of why they decided to go back to work; how they chose the type of childcare and whether it proved satisfactory; the reaction of employers and work colleagues; the role of husbands and fathers.

A picture emerges of compromise, anxiety and stress, and underlines the lack of a co-ordinated support system for working mothers. Any working mother reading this book will be reassured that her emotions and fears are shared by many others, and that her feelings of inadequacy in attempting to cope with baby, work and home are totally unjustified in the context of the situation in Britain today.

Julia Brannen is a sociologist at the Thomas Coram Research Unit. She has two children. She has conducted research on marital and family relationships, mental health and help-seeking behaviour and is the co-author of *Marriages in Trouble: the Process of Seeking Help* (Tavistock) and co-editor of *Give and Take in Families* (Unwin Hyman). She is currently carrying out research on dual-earner households and is convenor of the Resource's within Households Study Group.

Peter Moss is a Senior Research Officer at the Thomas Coram Research Unit. He has three children. He has conducted research on children with mental handicaps and their families, pre-school services, residential care for children and the experience of becoming a parent. He is the co-author of *Nurseries Now* (Penguin), *All our Children* and co-editor of *Work and the Family* (Temple Smith). He is currently carrying out research with Julia Brannen on dual-earner households and is also co-ordinator of the European Childcare Network.

NEW MOTHERS AT WORK

Employment and Childcare

Julia Brannen & Peter Moss

UNWIN
PAPERBACKS

LONDON SYDNEY WELLINGTON

First published in Great Britain by Unwin® Paperbacks, an imprint of Unwin Hyman Limited in 1988

UNWIN HYMAN LIMITED
15/17 Broadwick Street, London W1V 1FP

George Allen & Unwin Australia Pty Ltd
8 Napier Street, North Sydney, NSW 2060, Australia

Unwin Paperbacks New Zealand Pty Ltd with Port Nicholas Press
66 Cambridge Terrace, Wellington, New Zealand

British Library Cataloguing in Publication Data

Moss, Peter
New mothers at work.
1. Mothers—Employment—Great Britain
I. Title II. Brannen, Julia
331.4'0941 HD6135
ISBN 0-04-612048-3

Typeset in 10 on 11 point Sabon by
Computape (Pickering) Ltd, North Yorkshire
and printed in Great Britain by
Cox & Wyman Ltd, Reading

CONTENTS

ACKNOWLEDGEMENTS

The book would not have been possible without the financial support of the Department of Health and Social Security who funded the research programme on which the book is based. First and foremost, we wish to thank the women who took part in the study for their generosity – for their time, energy and enthusiasm. Thanks are also due to the research team, especially those who took part in the interviewing – Gill Bolland, Ruth Foxman, Mary Baginsky, and Ann Mooney. Other members of the team also provided support – Sue Martin, Ted Melhuish, Eva Lloyd, Brenda Meldrum and Rose Vinelott. Especial thanks to Heidi Mirza who contributed imaginatively to the analysis of the material used in Chapter 5; to Jane Williams for her managerial and secretarial skills; and to Charlie Owen for help with computing. We are also grateful to other members of the Thomas Coram Research Unit and to the staff at Unwin Hyman, especially Esther Caplin, for their encouragement and support. The views expressed in the book are of course entirely our own. We have endeavoured to preserve the anonymity of our respondents.

INTRODUCTION

The study on which this book is based was originally called the Daycare Project, a title which concealed key participants, namely the parents of the children who were being looked after. The idea was to follow the experience of a group of women, who expected to resume their jobs within nine months of childbirth, and their children until they were around three years old. The study was unique at the start and continues to be the only research of its kind in Britain today.

THE BACKGROUND TO THE STUDY

One of the common myths about academic research is that it is neutral and objective. However, this study, like all other research, arose in a particular climate and was influenced by ideas current in British society, including political and government circles, the research community and parents themselves. Two debates form the background to the research. Firstly, whether mothers with young children should go out to work, and secondly, if mothers go out to work, should their children best be cared for by individuals (assumed to be mother substitutes) or in group care (nurseries)?

Both these debates take it for granted that the mother is the best person to care for a young child and that deprivation of her full-time care is harmful to the child. The expectation that mothering ideally ought to be an exclusive activity, incompatible with employment, has proved very resistant to change in post-war Britain. It may have become rather more acceptable for mothers to be employed, if they work part-time and return to work once their children are at school. But the fact remains that the great majority of the population, including mothers themselves, still disapprove of women who go out to work when they have a young child, and especially if they have a full-time job. Not surprisingly, few women follow this course of action.

Over the last 15 years or so, there have however been significant changes in consciousness about the rights of women. With the rise of the women's movement in the early 1970s, there has been a growing awareness of the inequalities between men and women, particularly in the world of employment. This debate contributed to new laws on equal opportunities in the workplace – the Equal Pay Act and the Sex Discrimination Act in 1975, and the Employment Protection Act in 1976. These laws were however weak in their original formulation and have proved to be so in their enforcement.

There has been a curious disconnection in Britain between the debate about equality between men and women and the debate about motherhood and whether mothers of young children should work. The debate about mothers has a much lower profile although it is motherhood, both in terms of women's potential for giving birth and the actual experience, that is probably the main reason for women's disadvantageous position in society. The separation of these two issues has been facilitated by the division of the public world of employment and politics, designated as predominantly male, from the private female world of parenthood and family life. For the failure to connect these two worlds – the ways in which we separate them in our heads as well as in time and space – serves to marginalise the debate about working mothers and separates it from the wider debate about equal rights. However the women's movement, although it may have achieved few widespread changes in the way people live their lives, is changing the nature of the wider political agenda. Most of all it has revealed family life and motherhood as areas not only of great ambivalence for women but as being at the heart of women's material inequality both within the family and the public world beyond.

At government level these debates have had little effect. Issues around mothers' employment and parental employment (which does not even warrant the status of an issue) remain invisible in government policy. If anything the debate has moved backwards as the governments of the 1980s have adopted the approach of not intervening in 'family life'. They therefore consider issues like maternal employment to be outside the realm of government and in the province of private decisions. In their terms, they leave these matters to the market whilst at the same time taking legislative measures (for example tightening up on the qualifying conditions for maternity leave) which make the position of working mothers even more untenable. Likewise childcare provision has also been left almost entirely to market forces.

QUESTIONING ASSUMPTIONS

As the study progressed, our ideas have evolved and we have found ourselves questioning many of the assumptions that underlie much of the debate and research in this area of parenthood and employment. We have also come to understand more clearly the importance of certain issues. Two sources have been particularly valuable in furthering this process. Firstly, in 1981, the Government conducted a major survey on women's employment, the results of which, published from 1984 onwards, are a mine of invaluable information. Secondly, we have become more conscious of how these issues are viewed in other European countries and of the nature and extent of their childcare provision. Unlike Britain, many European countries – in Scandinavia in particular – have accepted that mothers of young children have the right to work. With the growth in the demand for labour in the 1970s they actively supported mothers' employment with various policies, including state investment in the provision of daycare services. Although the synchronisation of childcare with mothers' employment is far from complete in these countries the political will to provide childcare has to some extent enabled them to go hand in hand. This international perspective has made us increasingly aware of the importance of the wider social and political context which shapes attitudes to maternal employment and provision of childcare.

We have also become more aware of the impact of the first birth on women's labour market position, especially the long term negative effects on women's earnings and the major fall in the status of the jobs they frequently return to. The beneficial effects of paid work have become more apparent too: both the positive psychological effects on mothers and the significant financial contribution to the household economy which lifts many families out of poverty. Finally, it has been apparent to us from an early stage in the study that any examination of parental employment should focus on both parents, and not just on mothers; it should not be taken for granted that children are solely or even mainly the responsibility of mothers or that maternal care is necessarily best for children.

One of the ways in which we question traditional assumptions is to consider mothers' return to work in the context of the household, focusing on the distribution of work and responsibility between fathers and mothers in the dual earner lifestyle. But while our assumptions have changed since the study was planned at the end of the 1970s, our resources have not. We have had to be content with interviewing only the mothers and with exploring the fathers' role through mothers' eyes.

It is still the case that most mothers and fathers, including those in the study, believe that mothers should be responsible for children. So whilst we consider that a child has two parents and not just one, in practice the book tends to reflect the old order and to suggest that little has changed. Despite the fact that both parents in these dual earner households are in full-time employment very few have truly egalitarian partnerships. This is hardly surprising given the lack of egalitarian role models or of widespread discussion of these issues. 'Good' motherhood dictates that women, whether they are in work or not, should still take the major responsibility for the child, the home, and for making and maintaining the childcare arrangements. Our hope is that we have at least questioned and not simply taken these matters for granted.

THE STUDY

Our research is about households in which both parents are in full-time employment following the birth of a first child. It is also about the experience of using different types of daycare: the parents in the study used one of three types – relatives, childminders or nurseries. The main focus, however, is on the experiences of mothers going back to work – mostly on a full-time basis – within nine months of having a first child. (Although we use the term 'going back to work' to refer to women's resumption of their jobs, we do not intend to imply that childcare and other forms of domestic labour do not involve 'real work' – the term 'employment' is cumbersome to use every time.) The Employment Protection Act gives women who qualify the right to reinstatement in their former jobs – or similar ones – after maternity leave. Since 90 per cent of the women in the study went back to work within the terms of the maternity rights legislation, this book is in some respects a testimony to women's experience of the effects of this law.

We aimed to interview women before they resumed employment so that we could examine their decisions and circumstances while they were on maternity leave. We went back to interview the women within a few months of their return and on two further occasions. Essentially this book is about the material from the first two interviews. The story is in two parts: the story before and the story shortly after the return to work.

We chose to focus on women who had given birth for the first time. Although it is true that in general women suffer more disadvantages than men at school and in jobs and training after school, the point at which they give birth for the first time is critical for their subsequent careers. For various reasons – including the limitations of statutory maternity leave, strong social disapproval and the almost total absence of publicly-funded childcare for young children – going back to work after this event is rare in Britain. Having a first child is therefore the first time that most women have a break from the labour market. For women who leave their jobs to bring up their children, this break represents the point at which earnings and occupational status take a major downward turn. One aim of the study was therefore to examine the consequences for women of continuing in the labour market, in the same jobs, at this critical point of their lives.

Choosing the women for the study

As well as focusing on those with first babies we decided to study households where the parents were living together at the start of the study. We also selected women who were born in Britain and those living in the Greater London area. Our study does not therefore include all types of women who are likely to resume work; it specifically excludes single parents and non-British born mothers. This decision was a particularly controversial one within the research team. It was however decided to impose some limits on the sample.

Since one aim was to study children in three types of childcare – relatives, childminders and nurseries – we also had to select some women intending to use each type of childcare. Furthermore, we tried to strike a balance between women in professional and managerial jobs and those in clerical, secretarial, sales and manual work.

Because it was difficult to find women who definitely expected to resume work and who fulfilled all our criteria we had to pick up participants over a period of 18 months, between February 1983 and September 1984. To do this, we used three main sources: private nurseries, employers and maternity hospitals. Because nursery provision for the very young children of working parents is so rare we sought this group through the nurseries. Local authority nurseries were automatically excluded because they do not cater for children from two parent households who need daycare because their parents are employed. After a careful search, we eventually located only 33 nurseries in the whole Greater London area which took very young children, that is nine months or younger: 21 of these nurseries were attached to places of work. Altogether 98 names were given to us by these nurseries, of new admissions of very young children, which provided 35 women who fitted the research criteria. Our difficulty in finding parents who use nurseries clearly illustrates how remote are the chances of finding a nursery place for a baby.

Most of our other 'referrals' came through maternity hospitals and employers. Forty seven large-scale employers of women were asked to pass on names of women on maternity leave. Women were visited on the maternity wards of seven large hospitals and asked if they would mind being contacted again. Both groups of women were then telephoned (or written to) about 10 weeks after giving birth and asked about their work intentions, and were contacted again a few weeks later to arrange interviews if they fitted the research criteria. We had 4,100 'referrals'. The great majority were not intending to resume full-time work and many of the rest did not meet one of our other criteria. This left 295 women who were invited to participate in the study and 255 took part in the first interviews.

Researchers are inclined to impose order on their work; they aim to produce neat research designs, and like to have equal numbers of individuals in the groups between which they make comparisons. The real world is not an orderly place however. We were unable to divide our sample equally between parents using different kinds of daycare or to distribute these groups equally according to the different occupational groupings of the mothers. In fact the size of the groups that we ended up with reflects what we know about the real world of childcare use with some accuracy, with the exception of mothers in manual jobs. For example, our relatively small group of nursery users are mainly in professional and managerial jobs, a pattern confirmed by American, French and Swedish evidence. By contrast the group using relatives to care for their children contains few women in professional and managerial jobs, a finding which fits with the national picture of childcare use. In the event several women in the study used other types of childcare (for instance, in two cases fathers and in three cases a nanny) which were outside the remit of the research (see Table 0.1).

Because the study was structured around different types of daycare use we did not aim to produce a nationally representative sample of women going back to work. However if we compare our study with the available national evidence on women resuming work within a year of giving birth we find that our study has a much lower proportion of women in manual jobs. One reason for this was that 'referrals' from employers, a major source of participants in the study, consisted of women on maternity leave. Women in manual jobs are much less likely to qualify for maternity rights; if they do return to work within months of childbirth they usually return to new jobs.

The Interviews

The interviews were conducted with 185 women who intended to return to full-time work. They were first done when the children were four to five months old and before most of the mothers actually went back. The second interviews were carried out approximately five to six months after the return, when the children were 10 to 11 months old. We also interviewed a much smaller second group of mothers, 70 in all, who intended to adopt the traditional course of action and to stay at home with their children at least for the first year. (We make particular reference to these mothers in Chapter 3 where we consider women's experiences of being at home in the first months after birth.)

The first interviews were conducted in women's homes, except in one or two cases where the women had already resumed their jobs and where they preferred to be interviewed at their workplace. All the interviews were tape recorded and the bulk of the comments was subsequently transcribed by the researchers. Most of the interviews were lengthy, varying from one and a half to four hours. This was not only due to the fact that women had to break off to see to their babies. The first interview covered a great many areas including material about the past; women's work histories and their attitudes and feelings about having children, for example. It covered in detail the decision to return and the process of finding childcare. The same questions and topics were covered with each person but everyone was given ample opportunity to expand at length on their answers. Most women talked freely about themselves especially their worries about 'leaving' their children. Some women mentioned that this interview was one of the few opportunities for talking over these matters in any depth and that they found it helpful to do so.

The second interviews, conducted within a few months of the return to work, were done under more difficult circumstances. Many women were still exceptionally tired and, because they were working full-time, most had to be interviewed in the evenings. Some women managed to see us at work in their lunch time or during working hours if their employers were amenable – some were and others turned a blind eye. A number of women took a day or half a day's leave to see us. Given their very full schedules and the fact that they were tired it is surprising that they agreed at all to these visits. But almost everyone did and gave us at least a couple of hours of their time.

Moreover they continued to see us on several more occasions over the subsequent two years. Women were visited again when their children were 18 months and three years. Apart from the second interviews, most households received more than one visit at each of the four stages of the study. The children were assessed and observed both in their homes and at the carers'.

Parents (fathers were included here) were also required to fill in lengthy questionnaires and diaries about their children. Most agreed to take part; only 14 per cent of those initially asked to participate refused or couldn't be contacted and very few dropped out in the course of the study (only five people between the first two interviews). The response was therefore very good indeed, especially given the enormous demands that the research put on the families in the three years.

In making sense of the interviews our approach has been to stick closely to what women actually said to us. Since our questions aimed to tap women's own experiences we trust that we have represented them fairly and accurately. Our task as researchers is not however simply to reflect individual histories. We are also concerned with characterising the experience of the group and exposing patterns within collectivities or groups – we want to represent both the similarities and differences in women's experience of going back to work. To this end, the interviews were analysed in two ways. Firstly, we analysed answers to single questions by everyone in the study. Thus we were able to say how many people gave a particular type of answer to a question. We have avoided putting exact figures in the text: those who are interested should consult the tables in Appendix I. In addition we examined 70 cases in great depth: the quotations are drawn from these. We have drawn on these cases to exemplify the experiences of the women in the study.

OUR AIMS

Research is neither neutral nor objective. It is conducted by individual researchers who bring to their work perspectives and beliefs shaped by class, gender and race, as well as personal circumstances and experience. These perspectives and beliefs influence how researchers define the issue to be studied, how they interpret their data and the conclusions they draw from it.

Both of us have a strong personal investment in the work as well as an academic interest. Julia started out as a traditional British mother, staying at home with her two sons in their early years with no career waiting in the wings to return to. After becoming involved in the women's movement she retrained in social research methods and joined the labour market to carve out a career as a full-time researcher. Her part in the project was fostered by considerable curiosity as to how women who don't withdraw from the labour force fare when they have babies to look after as well as jobs to go to. Peter's involvement coincided with his decision to immerse himself in fatherhood and take a greater share of the responsibility in the upbringing of his third child. To do this, he cut down his working week, until his child started at nursery school. The demands and stresses of combining parenthood and employment, when there is a young child in the household, were very immediate to him during the early stages of the study, and he was particularly interested in the response of other fathers to these demands and stresses.

The book is also influenced by several beliefs, shared by both of us, two of which are particularly important. Firstly, it is our belief that childcare is not only mothers' business: it is also other people's – fathers' and society's in general. Secondly, women ought to have the right to economic independence. If, as seems to be the case, withdrawal from the labour market entails a long term and significant drop in their lifetime's earnings and employment opportunities, then women should be able to stay within the labour market whilst also becoming mothers. This requires adequate support both during maternity leave and over their return to work.

We hope that the book will give readers a clear idea of what it is like to go back to work in Britain under the present circumstances. The very fact that so few women do so in itself shows how hard it can be. It is not therefore surprising that the stories women tell are not particularly positive ones. On the other hand most are not particularly negative either. There is a stoic acceptance on the part of many women in the study that where problems arise it is up to them individually to find solutions. Where problems don't arise – where their individual strategies for finding childcare, for example, are successful – women regard themselves as lucky.

Just as people differ in the way they interpret their situations so they also differ in the resources available to them. By resources we mean financial and material support but we also mean social resources – for example, the availability of relatives to help with childcare. People also vary in their psychological resources; some individuals are amazingly adaptable and can surmount enormous difficulties against all odds. Others cannot.

We hope that by representing these women's experiences readers who are thinking about going back to work will be forewarned: that they will be alerted to the problems they may face and the ways in which other women have surmounted and come to terms with them. But we also hope that we have drawn attention to some of the *collective* solutions that are called for – in relation to employment practices for working parents, childcare provision and the sharing of childcare and domestic responsibilities. In forewarning future working mothers, we would also like to forearm them. We hope that at the very least the book will enable readers to be aware of some of the ways in which society could reorganise itself: both to enable people to combine parenthood with employment but also to make it a positive experience for both parents and children.

THE CHAPTERS

The book falls into two parts – before and after the return to work. Before launching into women's experiences we consider the social context in which women, in particular British women, resume work: we look at the facts and figures about motherhood and women's employment and how society expects 'good' mothers, fathers and workers to behave. The rest of the chapters are focused around the practical issues women face and how they are resolved. They are also about the feelings women experience both before and after the return; and the way others respond to mothers' predicaments and how mothers in turn feel about these responses. Key figures include fathers, bosses, work colleagues, mothers, relatives and the children's carers.

Chapter 2 is about the decision to continue in employment – who makes the choice and when, how and why those decisions are made. Chapter 3 is about women's experience of maternity leave and how they contemplate the return. Who made the childcare arrangements, and when and how the childcare was found is the theme of Chapter 4.

The second part of the book is devoted to the experience after the return. Since it is mothers who have had the break from employment we consider their experiences in the workplace once they are back, in Chapter 5. Chapter 6 is about how the childcare works out: the problems encountered and parents' satisfaction with the arrangements. Next follows an account of women's feelings when they leave their children in others' care and how combining full-time work with motherhood affects their well-being (Chapter 7). Chapter 8 is about how mothers cope: the practical strategies they employ for managing the dual earner lifestyle; the ways in which they mentally approach what they are doing; and the ways in which they deal with negative feelings. The penultimate chapter (9) looks specifically at the role of fathers in dual earner households. The concluding chapter points to some of the changes necessary to making maternity leave and returning to work a realistic possibility as well as a more positive experience for mothers.

CHAPTER 1

Putting it in context

The discontinuity in women's employment as a result of having children is an issue of central significance. It affects household income, putting households with young children at a considerable financial disadvantage, both in absolute terms and compared to other types of household. It leaves women financially dependent, and leaves them more vulnerable should their partner cease to provide. And it is a central factor in the creation of inequality in employment and earnings. Yet current social attitudes, reflected in a low level of practical support for working mothers, make it hard for women to choose to return to work.

THE EFFECTS OF MOTHERHOOD ON EMPLOYMENT AND INCOME

Only a handful of women remain continuously in the labour force throughout their childbearing and childrearing years. The general pattern in Britain is that women leave their jobs when pregnant with their first child. Few women – less than one in five – resume employment within nine months of having their first child. Even fewer go back to their previous full-time job within this period, and many of this small group eventually drop out for a period, often when they have a second child. After the initial break has been made, there may be spells of part-time work; but most women do not return to work permanently until their youngest child is at school, and then often only to part-time work. Recent research, based on the

'Women and Employment' survey, shows that the average woman having two children in her mid twenties will, as a result, lose six to seven years of employment.

The consequences for women of this pattern of discontinuous employment are enormous and lifelong. Many women are unable to resume the same level of job as when they left to have children; they often have to settle for the same work but at a lower level, or a different and typically less skilled job. Even should they get back to where they were, their colleagues will have progressed – in terms of experience, training, promotion and pay – in the interim; it will be difficult, and probably impossible, to catch up.

There is also a long term and adverse impact on income. Using the 'Woman and Employment' survey again, it has been calculated that a woman earning £6,000 a year (roughly the level of a junior secretary) when she has the first of two children in her mid twenties will lose £135,000 in earnings over a lifetime as the result of taking a break at this point. Women may lose money in three ways. Women lose earnings while they are unemployed. They lose earnings while they are working part-time, which women with children are far more likely to do. Finally, once back at work, women earn less because they have lost work experience and all that goes with it, such as increments, promotion and accompanying pay increases. Few employers regard women's experience in raising children and managing a house as relevant and valuable experience.

When a woman leaves paid work to have her first child, she usually becomes financially dependent on her male partner. She assumes that he will continue to provide for herself and her children until she goes back to her job. Over recent years, this has become an increasingly unsafe assumption to make. The increase in unemployment seems to have hit men with children more than other men, so that fathers now have above-average unemployment rates; in 1985, 12 per cent of men with children under 10 were out of work. Even more significant is the high level of marriage breakdown, with one in three marriages likely to end in divorce at current rates. Faced by the loss of a male provider, a woman who has left the labour force will either have to depend on social security or do her best to support herself and her children by finding a job, at which point her break in employment will put her at a major disadvantage.

THE EFFECTS OF MOTHERHOOD AND EMPLOYMENT ON WELL-BEING

Much has been written about the effects of mothers working on the well-being of both women and children. In very general terms, the conclusions are the same in both cases. There is no clear-cut relationship between the well-being of mothers or children and whether or not the mother is employed. Generalisations are likely to be unsafe and misleading.

Three factors are likely to affect the well-being of employed mothers. One is the type of work they do. Women who work in certain types of low paid jobs, where they have little control over their work, report poor physical health. By contrast those who work in better jobs where work is seen as a challenge report better health. Secondly, whether or not mothers *want* to work affects how they feel. Thus mothers who work when they don't want to are more distressed than those who are happy with what they are doing. Conversely mothers who don't enjoy being at home are more unhappy than those who enjoy it. Thirdly, the level of responsibility and the amount of work to be done affect well-being. Working mothers are at risk of what is known as 'role conflict' and 'role overload' – in short they may have too much to do. Whether or not this is a problem depends on the support available.

THE SOCIAL CONTEXT

Women's feelings about what they are doing are important, as are the actions, attitudes and responses of people with whom women are in regular contact – husbands, relatives, work colleagues and bosses. We consider both these factors in Chapter 9. In the rest of this chapter, we examine a third factor: the value and support society attaches to particular courses of action and how it expects people to behave.

This social context plays a crucial role in determining whether women do go back to paid work after maternity leave and, if they do, what they and their children then experience. The social context in Britain at the end of the 1980s is harsh and unsupportive for mothers who wish to work: it makes life unnecessarily difficult and stressful for many of them, and for their children. This is the bad news. The good news is that things do not have to be this way.

Important aspects of the social context, such as attitudes and services, can be changed to make it a source of positive support. We end the chapter by describing two countries where some attempt is being made to achieve this.

The 'good' mother

A central feature of this social context is the 'social construction' of motherhood. The term 'social construction' may be rather off-putting; but it is useful and worth keeping. For it emphasises that there is no universal, objective definition of what it means to be a 'good' mother; instead, a definition is constructed from the ideas, values and assumptions current in a society at any one time. So, what it means to be a 'good' mother is entirely relative. Even in the same society, at the same time, not everyone shares the same view about what being a 'good' mother entails.

Often, though, one view is particularly influential, dominating others. This is the case in Britain in the 1980s. This view, put at its simplest, is that mothers are mainly responsible for the care, development and well-being of children. To meet this responsibility adequately, mothers should give up paid work as soon as they have their first child, to look after their children on a full-time basis until the youngest is at least three years old. A 'little' job, for a few hours a week, may be acceptable if it doesn't interfere with mothering duties, and especially if it is done in the home, or during the evenings or weekends when perhaps the father can look after the children.

Before children reach the age of three, exclusive care by mother is best. To share the care with others, especially with a nursery, childminder or someone else who is not part of the close family, is to be avoided if at all possible and is not good for the children. A playgroup or nursery class is good for a child aged three years or more, but only for two or three hours a day at the most – and preferably with the mother regularly involved.

This socially constructed view of motherhood has evolved over the years, placing greater expectations and demands on women. That she should be actively involved in playgroups, nursery classes and other services for her child has already been mentioned. She should also spend time reading or watching an increasing volume of magazines, books, television programmes and videos which offer 'expert' advice and guidance about how to maximise her child's development and well-being. Her responsibilities in this respect have also expanded with the years. At the beginning of the century, attention was focused on the child's physical health and welfare. Subsequently, this has broadened to include the promotion of all aspects of the child's intellectual, social and emotional development. Today's 'good' mother is therefore expected not only to nurture her children, to show them affection and solve their problems, but also to help them develop to their fullest potential in all ways. The responsibility should the child fail to achieve this potential rests with the mother.

Women who resume employment after maternity leave transgress this idea of the 'good' mother in several basic ways. Not surprisingly, their choice is widely disapproved of. Over 80 per cent of both men and women in the 'Women and Employment' survey held that a married woman with a pre-school child should either stay at home or go out to work only if 'she really needs the money'. None said that 'she ought to go out to work if fit' and only a small proportion supported the proposition that 'it's up to her whether to go out to work or not'.

The 'good' father

A complementary 'social construction' defines the 'good' father. His main responsibility and task is to be the breadwinner, providing materially for his wife and children. Again, the basic concept has evolved somewhat over the years. The 'good' father is now also expected to be present at the birth of his children. He takes some time off work at this stage – probably when his wife gets home from hospital – but not too much, usually less than two weeks. He 'helps out' in the home, not so much with the housework, but with the children. He plays regularly with them, and may look after them sometimes by himself for a few hours and do some physical caretaking when the need arises. His main task though clearly remains to bring home the money; anything else is subsidiary to this main purpose.

The 'good' worker

A third 'social construction' defines the 'good' worker. This meshes with the definition of a 'good' father, enabling men to combine being a 'good' father and worker with a minimum of conflict and overload. 'Good' workers in 'proper' jobs work full-time. They have a continuous record of employment until retirement, with no voluntary breaks for personal or domestic reasons. They do not allow domestic or other 'private' responsibilities to intrude into their employment, except on the rarest and most extreme of occasions, such as at childbirth or in the event of a death or severe illness in the immediate family.

It might be argued that such a description is a travesty. Many workers have part-time jobs, at least at some stages in their lives. Many workers move in and out of work. This pattern is, however, frequently characteristic of women and women's jobs and is strongly associated with poorly paid, low skilled work, or at least work with low status attached, with few if any training, promotion or other opportunities for progress and development. The best employment opportunities are 'proper' jobs – fulfilling, rewarding and secure. These are most likely to be taken by men, who have to conform to the pattern of work expected of the 'good' worker.

The sad but true story of maternity leave

The tenacity with which the male dominated pattern of work is defended is demonstrated by the history of maternity leave legislation. Until June 1976, when the relevant section of the Employment Protection Act came into operation, the fact that nearly all women at some stage in their lives gave birth, and that this requires a period away from employment to ensure the health of mother and child, was not officially recognised. It was assumed and accepted that women would and should leave the labour market for some time at this point. A minority of employers operated their own maternity leave schemes; but there was no legislation to protect the interests of all women and children.

It took a long time for such a fundamental right, directly affecting half the adult population, to be recognised in law – and even then, the recognition was, and remains to this day, very partial. Incredible as it may seem, in Britain in the 1980s women still do not have a universal, legally enforcable right to maternity leave. For the measure introduced in 1976 imposed a highly restrictive qualifying condition requiring women to have worked for at least two years with the same employer. This 'length of service' condition excludes roughly half of all pregnant women from this most basic of entitlements. Moreover, rather than remove this condition, subsequent Government amendments have made the legislation more restrictive (see Appendix 2 for fuller details of these changes and current maternity leave legislation).

Other features of statutory maternity leave are equally inadequate. Less than half the period of leave – 18 weeks out of a potential 40 – is covered by any benefit payment. For 12 of these 18 weeks women get a low, flat-rate benefit; only for the remaining six weeks is their loss of income adequately compensated, at 90 per cent of earnings. At the end of maternity leave, there is no flexibility in how women may resume work. Unless they can do a deal with their employer, they must immediately resume at the same level of hours they worked before taking leave. No option exists, for instance, to start back on shorter hours, building back up to full-time, or to return on a part-time basis for a prolonged period.

The final part of this story is that maternity leave in Britain is not actually leave at all. Proper maternity leave provision would mean that women maintained their status as employees while absent from work, in the same way as an employee on sick leave or study leave. In Britain, the legislation is not framed in this way. Women on statutory maternity 'leave' actually have their contracts terminated, with a guarantee of re-employment in similar work; they have no entitlement to their previous job. While considered as employed for the purposes of National Insurance and state pensions, they do not have rights to non-statutory benefits, such as leave, bonuses, pay rises or promotion, during their absence.

The history of statutory maternity leave in Britain illustrates the powerful resistance to recognising employees' parental responsibilities, even in such a fundamental area as pregnancy and childbirth. Instead of a universal right, willingly granted as a step on the road to equality of opportunity for women, Britain has a partial entitlement, grudgingly granted, with no sense of commitment or belief in its rightness and importance. It is viewed by Government as, at best, a necessary evil to be kept to an absolute minimum and, at worst, as an obstacle to the workings of free market forces.

Childcare for employed parents

Progress on maternity leave entitlements has been minimal; on childcare it has been non-existent. No government since the war has tried to help employed parents with their childcare needs, either by subsidising parents' costs (for instance, via tax relief or a cash allowance) or the direct funding of services. Indeed, the most decisive postwar government action has been in quite the opposite direction. During the second world war, when women including mothers were expected to go out to work, the number of public day nurseries increased seven-fold in just three years. Once the war was over, they were rapidly closed, or converted into nursery schools; those remaining no longer admitted children of working parents (with the exception of single parents) and became instead welfare services for the children of families with major personal or social problems.

This change was justified on the grounds that 'good' mothers should not go out to work.

> The Ministers concerned accept the view of medical and other authority that, in the interest of health and development of the child no less than the benefit of the mother, the proper place for a child under two is at home with his mother. They are also of the opinion that, under normal peacetime conditions, the right policy to pursue would be positively to discourage mothers of children under two from going out to work.
>
> (Ministry of Health circular 221/1945).

This position was confirmed in a 1968 circular, which has remained the official position under both Labour and Conservative governments.

> Day care ... must be looked at in relation to the view of medical and other authority that early and prolonged separation from the mother is detrimental to the child and that wherever possible the younger pre-school child should be at home with his mother, and that the needs of older pre-school children should be met by part-time attendance at nursery schools or classes.
>
> (Ministry of Health circular, 37/1968).

Both circulars show how closely postwar governments, of both political parties, have identified with prevailing 'social constructions' of motherhood. This identification has further led successive governments to back the development of part-time provision for children over three years old, in nursery classes and playgroups. Valuable though these types of provision may be, they neither meet, nor are intended to meet, the needs of working parents and their children.

As a result of this consistent policy, women who go back to work after maternity leave cannot expect to find any publicly-funded childcare provision for their babies. The one exception is single mothers who are one of the groups eligible for admission to council day nurseries. There are, however, few places: 33,000 in Britain in 1986, or less than one place for every 100 children under five. In recent years children of single employed parents have been less likely to get a place than other groups, such as children thought to be 'at risk'.

Some employers make childcare provision, for instance in nurseries at the workplace or more rarely by subsidising places in other nurseries. There are, however, only 2,000 to 3,000 places for children under five in the whole country, and only a few hundred places for babies. The great majority of employers make no provision, and those that do are mostly in the public sector. This situation has been worsened by the government's decision in 1984 to tax parents who use a workplace nursery which is subsidised by their employer, the subsidy being regarded by the Inland Revenue as a taxable benefit.

This leaves a very limited number of childcare options. The most common type of care – accounting for just under half the pre-school children whose parents work full-time – is provided by relatives, particularly grandmothers. While this is often a very satisfactory arrangement, it is not always available, nor is it what all parents want.

The only generally available and relatively inexpensive form of childcare is childminding. Not surprisingly, this is the second most commonly used type of care. It accounts for about a quarter of pre-school children whose parents work full-time. Nurseries contribute to the care of about 15 per cent of these children, but less than five per cent of children under one year of age. There are some 30,000 places in private day nurseries, again less than one for every 100 children under five. Disproportionately few of these places are for babies or toddlers under two years old. The extra cost of caring for this very young age group acts as a disincentive, since it is difficult to provide good quality services for children of this age at a price that most parents can afford. Nannies and shared nannies are other possibilities, but are likely to be too expensive for many families.

Childcare – private or public?

Weak maternity leave legislation and the absence of publicly-funded childcare for working parents reflects the dominant ideas about how mothers should behave. In recent years, and especially since 1979, this lack of support for working parents has been sustained by the idea that the care of children is essentially a private matter. If parents wish to work, then it is up to them to make arrangements for their children's care. If benign employers wish to support employed parents, through providing childcare, better maternity leave provision or whatever, that is to be welcomed. Under no circumstances, however, is it the government's job to intervene in these matters; the government should 'interfere' in the family and the labour market as little as possible.

This view was being expressed in the 1970s by Conservative MPs, then in Opposition, when maternity leave legislation was going through Parliament. Then, they welcomed the principle of maternity leave, but argued for the introduction of a non-legal Code of Practice rather than legislation because 'traditionally (maternity leave rights) are matters for voluntary arrangement and it would be best to leave them for voluntary decisions'. More recently, the Conservative government has used the same argument to veto an EEC proposal on parental leave arguing that 'these matters are best dealt with between employers and employees according to their priorities, needs and circumstances and what they can afford'.

A EUROPEAN PERSPECTIVE

Women in Britain who go back to work are widely disapproved of and find little or no support from state or employers. How typical is this of other countries?

It is perhaps hardest of all to compare ideologies. The view that women with young children should not go out to work, but devote themselves full-time to their children's care finds support in most countries. It is perhaps as dominant as in Britain, or nearly so, in Ireland, the Netherlands and Germany. It is however less influential elsewhere. In Sweden, Denmark, France and Belgium, for instance, there is now widespread acceptance of women working when they have young children, and of the idea that even very young children can benefit from the experience of shared care, whether or not their parents work. The difference in attitudes is perhaps best illustrated in France, where as well as a substantial amount of publicly-funded childcare for working parents, there is a publicly-funded system of childcare – *halte-garderies* – where non-employed parents can regularly leave their children from a few months of age.

Comparing policies and services, we are on firmer ground. Maternity leave in Western Europe is generally shorter in duration than in Britain (ranging from six weeks post-natal leave in the Netherlands to 14 weeks in Denmark). It is however genuine leave, and it attracts for its full duration, both before and after birth, a high level of benefit of between 70 and 100 per cent of earnings. No other country has the sort of highly restrictive 'length of service' conditions found in Britain; in broad terms, statutory maternity leave is available to all employed women who become pregnant.

In addition to maternity leave, some form of statutory parental leave (see Appendix 2 for an explanation of parental leave) is now available in 10 of the 15 countries in the EEC and Scandinavia. These relatively new entitlements often leave a lot to be desired, usually because they are unpaid or paid only at a low rate, which increases the likelihood that they will be used exclusively by women. They are however a beginning.

Compared with most Western European countries where statistics are available, Britain has one of the lowest levels of publicly-funded childcare for the under threes (see Table 1.1). Moreover, half of the provision in Britain consists of places in nursery education occupied by two year olds, very largely on a part-time basis of 2–3 hours a day during term time. Publicly-funded places in day nurseries or with child minders account for just one per cent of under threes. It should also be added that, unlike Britain, all other European countries, with the exception of Ireland, include children of working parents as a priority for admission to publicy-funded childcare services.

A final point of comparison is employment rates. Employment rates are low among women with young children in Britain. While just over a quarter of women with children under five years old have jobs in Britain, the figure is touching, or has passed, the 50 per cent level in a substantial number of other countries (see Table 1.2).

Furthermore, not only do more women with young children have jobs in other countries, but they generally work longer hours; higher proportions work full-time, and part-time jobs on average involve more hours per week.

Denmark and Sweden

In these two countries, government policies to support employed parents are more fully developed than in any other country, certainly in Western Europe. In both countries, more than 80 per cent of women with children under three years are employed; 40 to 50 per cent of these working mothers are in full-time jobs. This implies that most women in these two societies now work continuously, except for maternity and parental leave, throughout their childbearing and childrearing years. A further important feature of both societies is that issues concerning childcare and parental employment have been and continue to be the subject of much discussion and debate. They are on the public agenda in a way that is totally lacking in Britain, where politicians, for instance, rarely give these issues a first, let alone a second thought.

Denmark offers 14 weeks of post-natal maternity leave, followed by a further 10 weeks of leave that can be divided between parents, in a two parent household, as they choose; both periods of leave are covered by benefit payments at 90 per cent of earnings. The most striking feature of Denmark however is the extensive system of publicly-funded childcare available for children from a few months of age upwards, which is mainly used for children whose parents are at work. Of children under three years, 44 per cent are in publicly-funded childcare services, either in nurseries or with childminders employed by the local authorities. Parents are charged on a means-tested basis, but the greater part of the cost is financed by government. As a result of this system, the pattern of care for children with working parents in Denmark is radically different to that in Britain. Two-thirds of children under three with working mothers are in publicly-funded childcare services, compared to less than five per cent in Britain. Relatives and private childminders, the most widely used types of care in Britain, account for less than a fifth of Danish children.

Sweden also has far more publicly-funded childcare than Britain. As in Denmark, this provision includes both nursery care and childminders recruited and paid by local authorities. An interesting variant (also now found in Denmark) is the three household scheme, where three families get financial support to employ someone to look after their young children in one of the family homes. Since the early 1970s, there has been a rapid increase in public funding – nursery provision, for instance, increased more than sixfold from 1969 to 1984 – and the current policy is to make childcare available by 1991 to all children between 18 months and six years whose parents want it. Sweden however is still some way behind Denmark in levels of publicly-funded childcare.

Sweden has however gone further than Denmark, or indeed any other country, in developing extensive leave entitlements for employed parents. After the birth or at any time up to the child's fourth birthday, 12 months leave can be taken. In two parent families, this can be divided between the mother and father as they choose, or can all be taken by one parent. Post-natal maternity leave, only for women, has been replaced by parental leave, equally available to mothers and fathers. This leave may be taken full-time or part-time; for example, if taken as half-time leave, the duration is doubled. Nine of the 12 months is covered by a benefit equivalent to 90 per cent of earnings, while the remaining three months is covered by a flat-rate benefit.

The other important leave entitlement in Sweden is for employed parents who have sick children or need to take children to medical or similar appointments. For these purposes, parents are entitled to 60 days paid leave per year per child under 12. A further two days paid leave per year is provided to parents to visit their children's nurseries or schools.

Underlying the development of policies in Sweden are several important principles. That women with children have a right to work, and that the State has an interest and responsibility in the area of parental employment is implicit in everything that the Swedes have done. More explicitly, there is a clear commitment to equality for women, and a belief that fathers should be equally responsible for children and that employment practices and patterns should recognise that men and women at work have children and responsibilities towards them.

CHAPTER 2

Deciding to go back to work

> I wasn't sure when I left whether I'd return. I just didn't know. It was going to be a complete change of life. When I had the baby I felt very much at a loss to know what to do with the little baby. I thought 'Wouldn't it be nice to go back to school?' – to the safe environment I knew ... You don't realise what a peculiar position you are in being a woman. You can take two completely different turns in life. When you're doing one thing you are always wanting to have a foot in the other camp.
>
> (*Primary school teacher, aged 35, who hasn't yet made up her mind whether to return*)

Deciding to go back to work after childbirth is a complex process. In this chapter we discuss why and when decisions are made and what and how women decide. The reasons women give involve internal motivations and external constraints: women go back to work because of financial pressures but they may also prefer having a job to being at home. Choices are made over time and in relation to the process of becoming a mother. Women begin to think about resuming work even before they get pregnant but they only finally decide after the birth, once any uncertainty surrounding the child and the childcare has been removed. As well as being a result of the past, decisions involve projections into the future: some women intend to continue working in the foreseeable future while others expect to give up within a few months or to become part-time. Plans can be made with or without reference to other people. Since mothers view children as primarily their responsibility, they see the choice not to care for them on a full-time basis as their own. The decision is largely an individual one; it is seen as the woman's choice and the woman's problem.

WHY WOMEN WANT TO GO BACK TO WORK

For women in less well paid jobs – clerical, secretarial and manual work for example – money is more often than not the main and only reason for going back to work. Women in professional and managerial occupations are more likely to return for other reasons, usually to do with personal preference, although they frequently mention financial pressures as a secondary factor (see Table 2.1).

Four cases are considered below. In the first two, finances are uppermost in the women's minds. But for financial constraints, both might well have given up their jobs at least for a while. In the last two cases, the women dwell on the importance of employment in their lives and feel they have a greater element of choice in the matter. Both women would prefer to continue working whatever their financial circumstances.

ALICE

A 29 year old hospital pharmacy technician, Alice has been married for four years to a porter in the same hospital. She says that although the pregnancy was not planned the child has arrived at the 'right time'. They have been buying their semi-detached house since they got married. They bring home similar incomes though the husband's earnings include a substantial amount of overtime. Though Alice has always expected to continue working there are times when she wishes she didn't have to go back to her job.

> If I wasn't working, about two weeks of my husband's salary would go on the mortgage. We wouldn't have an awful lot to live on and I'm one for buying clothes for the baby. I'm not good at keeping my money. I tend to spend it. And we've accepted a certain standard of living and are not really prepared to drop below it. In a way it's a selfish reason isn't it?

In addition Alice worries that if she gives in her notice she may never get her job back, especially since her boss openly disapproves of the fact that her husband works in the same department. She is also encouraged to return because the hospital provides a creche for the children of its employees.

GILLIAN

She is a 32 year old executive officer in the civil service. Her husband is also a civil servant and though he too is an executive officer he is higher up the salary scale and takes home more money than she does. After five years of marriage they decided to move from the flat into a house in order to start a family. Whilst house hunting Gillian discovered that she was pregnant. In view of their plans this happened 'a little too early'. She has to return to work when the baby is only three months old.

> I hoped we'd get established in a house, but then I found I was pregnant ... This house is considerably more expensive than the one we'd hoped to buy. If we'd got the other one I could have been off work a lot longer – probably the full six months and possibly could have given up work and taken another job when Angela was one or two ... I would like to have worked so I could leave and then go back to another job perhaps after a year. I appreciated I would have to go back on a lower grade ... I always knew I would have to work, that we wouldn't be able to manage on one salary at least initially. We're hoping now that when Angela is 4 or 5 we'll have another baby and I will be in a position to stay at home or change to part-time. (*When did you decide to return?*) When we found this house and I knew I was pregnant and we couldn't afford the mortgage. There was just no way we could consider staying in the flat and have a baby ... And we've spent such a long time fixing the house up the way we wanted. So if we're going to be that greedy and self-indulgent we have to pay the price.

Alice talks about going back for financial reasons as being 'selfish' and Gillian mentions feeling 'greedy' and 'self-indulgent', as if only really severe financial straits were sufficient justification for going back to work when children are very young. Implicit in what they say is that only mothers ought to care for very young children.

ANGELA

A 29 year old teacher, Angela is married to a further education college lecturer who earns rather more than she does. Four years after marriage they decided to have a child and move to a larger house. Angela has always expected to work because she finds her job very absorbing. However, finances also play an important part.

> I have always worked. The prospect of staying at home I find quite daunting, even though I've got a lovely baby to occupy myself with. And I felt if I didn't go back to work now I might regret it later on. I might resent the baby for stopping me . . . My main reason was financial but that's easy to say because I do actually enjoy my work. (*What do finances mean?*) Well, when I got pregnant we had three old cars, a motorbike and we had just moved house. We decided we needed a new car and to get things for the house. We hadn't long moved. And when you move you end up with a whole pile of debts . . . And it's a lovely feeling that you're saving again . . . I mean a lot of people don't but that's the way you're brought up. You've got this goal to save. But that's not what I really mean by financial. Really it's paying off the loans and getting a new car.

MIRIAM

She is a 35 year old senior administrator who has worked her way up the career ladder, acquiring professional qualifications through day release and evening classes. She and her husband have similar jobs, work for the same large employer and earn the same salaries. They have been married for 13 years. Miriam deferred having a baby because she has been uncertain about how she could combine motherhood with her career. Fearing that later on she might regret not having children, they decided to start a family and move to a larger house in an upmarket area. They need two incomes to cover the increased mortgage and to keep up their standard of living at least in the short term. Miriam gives job satisfaction as her main reason for resuming work.

> I need the stimulation to fulfil myself. I think that's why I'm going back to work because if I stayed at home – though it may be best for the baby it wouldn't be best for me and so in the long

> run it wouldn't be best for him ... so my main reason is that I don't find staying at home sufficiently stimulating. I find my work challenging. I find I need that sort of stimulation to keep me going. I think in the long run it's better for the child to have me happy and contented when I am with him than at home possibly resentful because I'm not doing what I want ... Financial considerations are important to the extent that we have commitments we would find it a bit difficult to meet if I wasn't at work.

Financial reasons

Women make a major financial contribution to the household which almost equals their husbands' contribution. This is not surprising since most have been employed continuously since leaving school, further or higher education and they have worked for almost as long as their husbands. On average they take home four fifths of their husbands' earnings and contribute 40 per cent of the net household income. In practice they spend their earnings on the same major items of household expenditure as their husbands do, including the mortgage and the bills. The only exception is childcare which they see as their financial responsibility and pay for either out of their own earnings or from the joint account (see Table 2.2).

Women not only make an important contribution, they also feel it is important to do so.

> I think there's a general feeling that is prevalent among all classes of women that you feel more obligation today to make some kind of monetary contribution to the household ... Because more women do work and you get so used to the money ... You get used to the lifestyle. You feel less guilty about spending money if you've helped to earn it. I certainly feel like that ... I feel much better if I know some of it is mine.
>
> (*Teacher, aged 26*)

Women are not happy with the prospect of being economically dependent on their partners. A few months on maternity leave is enough for most. Most women have tasted economic dependency for only a short time with many drawing on their personal savings in this time.

> (*How would you feel being financially dependent on your husband?*) Dreadful! ... And I don't mean because he doesn't earn that much. If he were a millionaire it would be the same. It wouldn't feel like it was your own money – like buying somebody a birthday present with the money they have given you. I know one shouldn't feel like that ... But I've always had this thing about being financially independent ... It goes back to my parents. The only way my mother made any headway was to go out and earn her own money ... I couldn't bring myself to rely on anybody else to provide me with what I want because you lose your freedom.
>
> (*Local government administrator, aged 31*)

Women do not go back to work to spend money on themselves: they see themselves as working for the 'family unit'.

> Spending money on myself is a very low priority. Since we've assumed the responsibility for having a house of our own it has altered. I obviously have less money to spend on myself though I never was a big spender.
>
> (*Teacher, aged 37*)

The arrival of a baby deflects attention away from women's personal needs, so much so that they develop guilt feelings about spending money on themselves. Becoming a mother arouses strong feelings of altruism.

> I'm not spending any money on myself. I try very hard not to. Obviously I have to buy things like tights. But clothes, I'm trying to survive on what I had before. But I did need a new coat and we agreed I could have one. (*How did you feel?*) I felt 'I wish I could have spent more'. I felt this was the most economical coat I could buy. (*Have you felt differently since you had the baby?*) Yes. I'm more cautious and I feel guilty. I feel I can't spend any money. It wasn't too much of a problem before.
>
> (*Laboratory technician, aged 36*)

Even though women's earnings, like those of their husbands, go on basic household expenditure women tend to view their respective financial contributions rather differently.

> I've felt it often. I suppose it's a matter of 'You're the man! You earn the money'. But it's not realistic really because I earn more than he does and we share the costs of everything. (*Why do you feel that way?*) It's my upbringing isn't it? Men are supposed to be the breadwinners. But I normally only think that when I'm pissed off with him for some reason ... Don't get me wrong, my money is crucial. We both recognise the fact.
>
> (*Doctor, aged 30*)

Since getting married most women have contributed to household expenses. Yet even if they put their earnings, as many do, in joint bank accounts they label their own money in their minds as having a particular significance, with a considerable number viewing it as a luxury or 'extra'. At the heart of this contradiction is the traditional legacy that the *man* ought to bring home the 'breadwinner wage'. This belief exists alongside the contemporary expectation that marriage ought to be about 'sharing'.

> (*How important do you think your money is to the household?*) It is important because it allows us to buy things for the baby and for ourselves which we would never do if I wasn't working. (*So you see your money as buying special things?*) No, not really. It's our money and we both share it ... But if we were just taking my husband's money into account it would hardly cover the bills. There wouldn't be an awful lot left to buy things – luxury things.
>
> (*Bank clerk, aged 30*)

Even in these dual earner households the old idea of women earning 'pin money' is still found though in a modified and subdued form.

Because of the strong belief in marriage as an equal partnership it suits women not to look too closely at whether each partner does in fact get fair and equal shares, especially since in practice women rarely do as well as men. By continuing to work after childbirth women don't have to calculate where every penny goes. They can afford not to know. Bringing in two incomes is therefore one important, often unconscious, strategy by which marital strains and conflict over money can be avoided. One woman, recently back at work, describes a relaxed approach to money in her own marriage:

> We don't have a lot of control over our money. If we've got it we spend it. We're not good at saving ... If one of us needs money we'll give it to the other. It's just our money ... It wasn't a conscious decision to do it this way. I've never wanted us to be divided about money. And I never wanted to get into a situation of thinking 'It's my money' or 'his money'.
>
> (*Telephonist, aged 30*)

Sally, on the other hand, is far from relaxed about money. She has the responsibility for budgeting and, because her husband is such a spendthrift, she now handles all the financial affairs. Several months after resuming work she decided to give up her job because she felt she ought to be at home with her child. Money is likely to become an even greater source of tension when she gives up work.

> The reason I make a fuss (about handling the money) is that I want my husband to be a bit more responsible for when it's only his wage that's coming in. (*How will you feel then when you're financially dependent on him?*) I'd rather I wasn't. And he did remark on it which I thought was hurtful really. We'd arranged to have a family and he'd agreed I could give up work. So I don't think he should have said that ... And I've always put my money into the bank. I've never really spent a lot of it ... So I can say I've put my share into the marriage when I've had the money ... But I'll just have to accept it really ... But I will miss my money.
>
> (*Clerical worker, aged 23*)

Women's accounts of financial pressures suggest that they come in a variety of guises. To say that one is going back to work for the money is a socially acceptable justification which does not invite further questions. Nearly everyone has some experience of financial problems although they clearly have different meanings in different economic contexts.

Women often talk rather vaguely about maintaining their 'standard of living'.

> I see it that we are able to live at a higher standard of living than what we would otherwise be ... I think one has to decide how one wants to live and at what standard one wants to live.

> And if you want to live at a certain standard you've got to work.
>
> (*Doctor, aged 32*)

At childbirth the household resources are threatened not only by a major drop in income if the woman leaves her job but also by the additional expense of a new person. Even if the woman plans to return to work, the birth coincides with the loss of almost half the household income. Only part of the 29 weeks statutory maternity leave after the birth is paid. During this time nearly one half of women mention some kind of financial problem which serves as a further justification for returning to work. Indeed, few women can afford to take the full 29 weeks statutory leave. One third go back by the time the child is five months old and one half by six months. On their return women have either used up or dug deep into their personal savings; others have gone into debt.

> I could have stayed off several months longer but financially I couldn't afford to because the money ran out ages ago ... Although we sort of share our money, we couldn't afford to live on my husband's wage.
>
> (*Teacher, aged 31, who returned to work when her child was three months old*)

For couples today decent housing is seen as the major precondition for starting a family. The importance of having your own house is increasingly central to ideas about a 'proper family life'; a family of one's own is ideally prefaced by a home of one's own. It is seen as irresponsible to have a child before you have set up house or achieved some degree of economic security. In fact although property ownership is high and still rising throughout the population, it is highest among those with very young children. Couples today, especially those living in London, are in a very difficult housing situation. Because of the high value that is placed on home ownership there is a shortage of accommodation available for rent. The London housing market is especially problematic, with exceptionally high and constantly accelerating house prices. Almost one third of the women interviewed mentioned housing as a main financial pressure.

> (*What were your main reasons for resuming work?*) Financial, to cover the mortgage and the standard of living really ... I

> wanted David to grow up in a fairly nice house and a fairly nice area rather than a council house somewhere . . . I mean I could have given up work and we could have moved into a flat. That would have worked. It would have solved the problem . . . I think of the money as the house's, the taxpayer's and David's at the moment.
>
> (*Radiographer, aged* 26)

These households all live in or around London and the great majority have taken out mortgages. Many have bought older properties some of which are in need of considerable repair and renovation. Some couples have taken out loans to cover housing improvements but most are carrying out the work themselves. In the expectation of parenthood many have only recently moved from a flat into a house or have moved to a larger house. They are often still paying off the cost of the move.

Other reasons

A considerable proportion of women, especially those in professional or managerial jobs, give personal preference as their main reason for going back to work. Women's accounts contain two interlocking themes – on the one hand, reasons for not wanting to be at home all the time and, on the other, reasons for wanting to work.

As described in the next chapter, many women are unhappy with the experience of being a housewife. Being on maternity leave really brings it home to them. Some give this as a major reason for resuming work. They feel it important 'to get out of the house', 'to have contact with people', to be 'mentally stimulated'. Dissatisfaction with being stuck at home all day is one key factor which *pushes* women back to work. Those with interesting and financially rewarding jobs are also likely to feel *pulled* back to work: they dwell on the fulfilment to be gained from work which is usually their main reason for returning.

> Personal satisfaction is as important as anything else. (*More important than finances?*) That was important but we could have survived. I mean I enjoy my work. That is the main reason for going back – that I enjoy it. And I enjoy the contact with

> other people there ... If I hadn't enjoyed my job I would probably have thought differently.
>
> (*Teacher, aged 30*)

Not surprisingly those in routine, poorly paid jobs dwell on the factors pushing them back to work – the negative experience of being at home – although they generally mention money as the more important consideration.

For women who invest a great deal of themselves in their jobs, especially if they have spent a lot of time training for them, employment forms a central part of their identities. Asked the question 'If someone said to you what do you do, how would you answer?' over two thirds of working mothers mention their occupations, compared with only a small proportion of mothers who stay at home. Some women fear that motherhood may entail a loss of identity: returning to work is therefore seen as a means of sustaining it.

> Sanity! (laughs) My real reason is that – I want to go back more because of what I don't want to become. That sounds very negative but, as I said before, I don't want to live for the children. I think that is very restricting for the child. Later I think he may respect the fact that you work as well – that you had other interests apart from him.
>
> (*Careers officer, aged 30*)

Women are only too well aware of the high value that our society places on paid work and the way it ignores women's largely invisible unpaid labour in the home. This lack of recognition can lead women to lose their self-respect after only a short spell at home.

> I do think I get a bit dull when I've been at home all day. When my husband comes home I haven't got an awful lot to say apart from what the butcher said to me and how much the baby weighed at the clinic. My converstion is pretty limited. Yes. So I think the stimulation of work and the self-respect. Whatever one thinks of being a mother – to be staying at home looking after a child is not valued. You are low status. People who know you don't judge you like that, do they? But the general feeling is that society doesn't value it. So I do feel a bit of a layabout.
>
> (*Language teacher*, aged 31)

There are psychological benefits to employment: not only does paid work enhance and protect self-confidence, self-esteem and self-respect, it also gives a sense of security and structure. Having a job has been shown to be one of the main buffers against poor mental health, especially depression. Many women are also aware that their own sense of well-being is likely to affect their children. If they feel happy in themselves, their children are likely to be happy as well. Conversely, if they feel dissatisfied with themselves and their lives, the children are likely to suffer.

WHEN WOMEN DECIDE

Five months after the birth, the women in the study talked about when they decided to go back to work. Whilst on maternity leave, nearly two thirds think that their intentions were already firm before the pregnancy, with the rest equally distributed between those who date their intentions from the start of the pregnancy and those who do so after the birth (see Table 2.3). For many, however, the decisions are only finally settled once a number of doubts and uncertainties about the birth, the child and the childcare are resolved.

After the birth

The pregnancy itself can be a turning point. Roughly a quarter became pregnant unexpectedly with most of these feeling that they had no choice but to continue working. Veronica, a 35 year old bank clerk, was in this position. She had recently remarried and had to start once again at the bottom of the housing ladder. Paying the mortgage depends on having two incomes.

> And I felt I was too old to have a child and there might be something wrong if I did. And we'd only been in this house for two years . . . I just didn't think there was a possibility of getting pregnant because I knew we couldn't afford for me to stay at home and look after a baby.
>
> (*Clerical worker, aged 35*)

Eventually Veronica went to her GP, a woman doctor, who confirmed the pregnancy and mentioned that she herself had returned to work after childbirth. Had the GP not given her the idea Veronica says she would have tried to obtain an abortion.

Other events which influence the timing of women's decisions include housing, an issue already mentioned. Some women have only recently changed jobs when they discover they are pregnant.

> I thought I would have to leave . . . I'd envisaged staying in that job for some time so it was a difficult decision to leave before I'd intended. I felt guilty because I had not been there that long.
>
> (*Senior laboratory technician, aged 31*)

Under these circumstances women do not qualify for maternity leave because the law requires women to have been with the same employer for two years. Those who return do so because their employers make a special concession.

Second marriages sometimes figure in women's decisions – for example if the father is required by his ex-wife to increase the financial support of his children by a first marriage. One woman in this situation is reluctant to confront the uncomfortable issue of maintenance. She dismisses the matter:

> I always knew I'd have to go back to work but I hoped I wouldn't. I expected I would have to.
>
> (*Nurse, aged 29*)

After the birth

In many cases the decision is gradual and only finally settled after the birth. In pregnancy many women talk about 'keeping their options open' meaning that they want the opportunity to return to their jobs in case anything 'goes wrong' at or after the birth. Maternity leave therefore offers one very basic advantage: it provides an insurance against mishap in childbirth which women would be ill-advised not to take up.

The child is a further consideration. Going back to work depends on the baby's temperament – is she the type of child who will settle easily in daycare? A final concern is the daycare itself. As will be discussed in Chapter 4, there are a number of constraints preventing women from booking their daycare too far in advance, especially childminders and nurseries. Only in the case of those using relatives, who tend to offer their help in the first months of the pregnancy, is the matter settled early on.

WHAT WOMEN DECIDE

Women on maternity leave view their return to work from a short rather than long term perspective. They do not necessarily intend to stay in the labour market, especially if they want to have another baby. One of the many complications they envisage is the escalating cost of childcare. Paying for two or more children out of their earnings means that it isn't 'worth their while' working.

Under the maternity leave legislation women are required to return to full-time work. Not surprisingly many women view their return tentatively. One of the main ways they cope with the uncertainty – with whether they will be able or want to continue working full-time – is to 'see how it goes'.

> I've decided I'll take it from April to October – say six months. And then see how I feel about staying. I've got to go back obviously but I don't know if it's going to be that easy. So I'll see how it goes. I might decide I don't want to carry on working after October.
>
> (*Clerk, aged 23*)

Some women envisage changing to part-time employment when their children start school and full-time childcare is no longer necessary.

The cost of childcare is a major consideration here especially since the calculations of whether they can 'afford' to work is based on their earnings and the amount of money left over after *they* have paid for childcare. They do not view this as a cost to be born by both working partners; fathers are not expected to contribute.

Mothers are seen to be the prime carers of children. If they decide to contravene the norm and go back to work it is assumed that they must find substitutes for themselves. Women are therefore conscious that they must 'pay a price': part of that price is the cost of childcare.

> Half of my money gets paid out on childcare and the lady who cleans the house. (*Is it because it's actually paid out of your earnings?*) I think it's to do with the fact that I work that it's

> down to me. Because we've got a joint account in theory it doesn't matter. But I class it as coming out of my money. (*Does your husband think that as well?*) Yes, I suppose he does. Because he talks about 'As long as we're not spending more than half your salary on these things, it's probably worth it'.
>
> (*Surveyor, aged 35*)

Women's decisions to return to work are usually made in the short term, often for financial reasons. They talk about staying in their jobs until they have paid off particular debts and loans, some of which have accumulated during their largely unpaid maternity leave. Other women talk about continuing to work – or to work full-time – until their partners are in a position to earn more. A few say they will stay in the job only as long as it takes to repay their maternity money, where this is a condition of reinstatement set by their employer.

Even those in professional or managerial jobs do not appear to have long term perspectives. They don't mention the financial or the other benefits of maintaining an unbroken career. In contrast, they take it for granted that their husbands, especially if they are in professional or managerial jobs, should be career oriented. As first-time mothers, especially within five months of the birth, they are preoccupied with their children and their new responsibilities as parents. They are still at home on maternity leave and are only beginning to reorientate themselves towards the world of employment. Although they intend to return full-time – many because they have to – and as yet have virtually unbroken employment records, they do not necessarily see themselves as continuing along this path.

Even those who intend to stay in full-time work envisage 'treading water' for a while; they do not intend to seek promotion while their children are very small. If they hope to change to part-time hours only a very few women express concern about the likely drop in status. No one talks about the advantages of continuing in their jobs in the event of divorce.

HOW WOMEN DECIDE

Most women having children in Britain assume they will give up their jobs toward the end of pregnancy and stay at home to look after their babies at least for their first years. For the majority this decision is simply taken for granted. By contrast, women who take up their right to return to work (if they have the right) are required to make a definite decision which challenges the status quo. This decision therefore represents not only an assertion of a woman's right but a rejection of the norm. Such decisions are not taken lightly.

> I think it takes great courage for a woman to go back to work. Even if she has gone back by choice, even if she wants to do it, it still takes great courage. I think women shouldn't be made to feel guilty . . . There's always this view 'You stay at home'.
>
> (*Hospital cook, aged 20*)

Women who resume work after childbirth see it as their 'choice' even though they may feel highly constrained by finances. This is because society *expects* them to give up work when they have a child. There is no question as to whether the father should give up his job.

Women's decisions are also largely personal. They are made with little reference to their husbands or to other people. In general, husbands only express firm opinions on the matter if they prefer their wives to look after the children at home. Nearly half express this preference; many 'sit on the fence'; others send out ambiguous messages. Thus even if there are pressing financial reasons for returning, women describe the onus of the decision as falling mainly on them.

> He's taken it for granted I'll go back. He's said it's up to me – do what I want to do. (But) I think he'd really like me to stay at home and look after her.
>
> (*Teacher, aged 28*)

Women do not complain about this state of affairs. In most cases they accept it. Since they see resuming work as their choice they accept responsibility for their decisions – as the price for challenging the status quo. None the less it can be a lonely experience.

> In the end it was my final decision that I made on my own, regretfully. I would have preferred someone to have forced me into it – no, I wouldn't. But it was a hard decision.
>
> (*Cook, aged 20*)

It is not that women want the decision to be taken out of their hands. What they feel the need of is joint responsibility for the consequences of these decisions and for the burden of childcare and domestic work (see Chapter 9).

CHAPTER 3

On maternity leave: thinking about the return

> (*What are the best things about being a mother?*) There are times I could wring his neck! But I think it's worth it in the end. I can't really say what I enjoy. I just enjoy being with him. I enjoy showing him off. I suppose I enjoy looking after him. But I don't like getting up to him in the night when he cries. Now I don't mind. I get up automatically. (*What are the worst things?*) Tiredness is the worst thing.
>
> (*Supermarket cashier, aged 22*)

Motherhood involves both losses and gains. The gains evoke powerful positive feelings and the losses strong negative emotions which together produce conflict and ambivalence. It is possible to feel deeply attached to a child, discovering great rewards in her or his mere existence, and yet at the same time to find the demands and constraints of being constantly on call tiring and frustrating.

THE PLEASURES OF MOTHERHOOD

Mothers who propose to go back to work love their children just as much as mothers who stay at home. But exactly what do they enjoy? First and foremost are the babies themselves. Mothers are rewarded by seeing their children grow and develop, by children's responsiveness and by the sensuousness of close physical contact with them. These rewards are immediate. Some mothers take pleasure in the child's dependence, despite the responsibility dependence entails, and they savour the power that goes with it.

> (*What are the best things about being a mother and looking after your baby?*) I don't know really. It's being able to give so much of yourself and the loving. And I find it fascinating just watching him develop – not knowing about babies and that I think is quite stimulating. It's a whole area I've never been involved with before.
>
> (*Solicitor, aged 29*)

> Well, the look of adoration you get and the way she smiles and wriggles up her whole body at you and you laugh at her – the total acceptance of you is probably the best thing.
>
> (*Secretary, aged 40*)

> I think having someone to depend on you. I think that's a lovely feeling. That's really nice. And I think *knowing* that when Jo smiles at me – knowing that I have the *power* to make him happy ... The way that each day he is growing. Each new thing he does is a revelation really. I think that is lovely.
>
> (*Hospital worker, aged 20*)

> Just the amount of joy it's brought and the feeling that other people give to me because of him ... Well, the way friends show concern over me and him ... When he was born everybody wanted to see him and me. I just felt very loved and I know he's very loved and I've been able to give so much love. It's something I've never experienced to such an extent before.
>
> (*Teacher, aged 37*)

> You just start seeing things through a little child's eyes – that is the main thing. You can be a bit of a kid yourself again. That's what I like. Going out and buying little toys and little clothes. Like the other day, we went to the park and showed him the ducks and his little face it was lovely to see. I can sort of be a little kid for the rest of my life really.
>
> (*Radiographer, aged 26*)

> I don't know what the best things are. It's lovely to see her when she smiles and to feel she's actually your own. The only thing you ever have that is actually something that's yours and no one else has had anything to do with.
>
> (*Careers officer, aged 34*)

The joys of motherhood represent an accumulation of these moments of pleasure and, in the process of reflection, motherhood is constructed as an enjoyable experience. In addition women hold on to the idea, fostered by baby books, professionals and by common sense beliefs, that 'it's all worthwhile in the end'.

THE PAINS OF MOTHERHOOD

Because mothers are told that motherhood is enjoyable they are somewhat reticent about the things they don't enjoy. Not surprisingly babies' temperaments have a considerable effect – whether they sleep at night or cry much during the day. It is increasingly recognised that babies' temperaments do affect their mothers' tempers and that it is not all the other way round. Four months after the birth over a third of all mothers complain of moderate or severe tiredness. Three quarters feel irritable with their children from time to time. These feelings often lead to a desire to get away from the wailing infant which conflicts with the strong sense of duty mothers feel towards their babies. Failure to comfort a crying child can induce feelings of frustration, inadequacy and sheer desperation.

> (*What are the worst things about being a mother?*) It's the crying – when I just can't find the particular key to shut him up. That drives me up the wall. I can understand why people batter babies. If you're on your own in a bedsitter I don't know how on earth you manage. Sometimes, I just think 'I just can't stand this any more – what am I to do with him'.
>
> (*Local government administrator, aged 35*)

> I think now – they're at a stage where you just can't please them. They can't do things for themselves. You've got to try and keep them amused. When they are tiny they go to sleep all the time.
>
> (*VDU operator, aged 22*)

Loss of identity

Becoming a mother affects how a woman sees herself and how she is seen by others. It can erode her sense of being a person in her own right. Mothers who intend to remain at home after childbirth also lose their identity as workers and see themselves principally as mothers and housewives.

How women feel about motherhood is closely bound up with the way society views it. While 'good' mothers are expected to stay at home little status is given to their work.

> (*What don't you enjoy about being a mother?*) I don't like the low social status and I don't like the unsociable hours. This thing – the fact that society doesn't value it. It's the thing of 'just being a mother – just being at home'. The feeling I have is that it is one of the most important things that people can do – being at home and being a mother ... I'm so wrapped up in feeling it's all wonderful ...
>
> (*Clinical psychologist, aged 30*)

In Britain becoming a mother involves loss of identity but also a loss in earnings. Even those on maternity leave are paid for only a short period. Finances have a major impact on the experience of being at home with a young baby, determining what mothers can afford to do and have – from putting on the heating to using disposable nappies. Finances also influence how women feel. Most first time mothers have worked continuously since leaving full-time education. Even if there is money to spare, women who are used to earning feel guilty about spending their husbands' income.

> The only thing was when I was on unpaid leave I didn't have so much money. I had a slight guilt feeling about going out and spending money and enjoying myself. Then I think 'Oh, my husband is at work'.
>
> (*Hospital administrator, aged 32*)

Conditions of work

Mothers returning to work are less positive about their experience of full-time motherhood five months after the birth than mothers who intend to remain at home. Over half feel moderately or highly dissatisfied – twice as many as those not intending to return (see Table 3.1). It is the working conditions of motherhood which give rise to a great deal of this dissatisfaction. Mothers complain most about the *full-time* nature of mothering: the domestic overload, the social isolation and restriction to the home, the boredom, monotony and sameness of life. With babies of five months most mothers feel tied down and in practice are in sole charge of their children 24 hours a day, seven days a week. A substantial number are restricted to the house with little adult company. The babies still need to be fed and changed at frequent intervals which can be monotonous, tedious and tiring, especially if it is the mother's responsibility alone.

Many mothers also acknowledge the positive aspects of full-time motherhood. Autonomy is the most valued feature: roughly half of women whatever their work intentions mention it. But 'being your own boss' is often more theoretical than real. It enables 'freedom from' rather than 'freedom to', releasing women from the less pleasant aspects of employment but providing few of the positive rewards. Paradoxically, though women say they like being 'their own boss' they also complain about having too little time, and being 'slaves to the housework'. Lack of time to themselves is something that women mind about a good deal but again women who return are more likely to be resentful.

Alison, a teacher, resumed work when her child was 18 weeks old. Although going back is a strain, especially since the baby is still very wakeful, she regards her time at home as unsatisfying. She has a large kin network but knows few people in the neighbourhood.

> (*What don't you enjoy about being a mother?*) It can make you very lonely. If my husband wasn't around I wouldn't see anyone all day ... And the frustration as well ... You feel frustrated that you can't do all the work – And I mean you want to get on with your own interests and you can't do them ... People tell you housework's not important and all the rest. But sometimes it does build up ... and you get tired and you nag ... I thought it would be nice (to be at home). I quite liked the idea of it. And then I hated it after. I went over to Ireland and when I came back, I was completely alone and I couldn't bear the thought of seeing nobody. Also, just being trapped in this awful room with her because of the state of the house. And I used to build up all these silly moans when my husband came

> in and tell him . . . The usual complaints of first time mothers at home. And then I realised that just to get away from the home could be a great break for me. I don't think he understood and nor does anyone else until they are in that position. You sound petty and you feel embarrassed at times moaning about a silly thing like being at home with the baby. I sympathise with anyone now. She just demanded attention 24 hours a day and you just feel you can't give it all the time . . . I think that was the worst part . . . the loneliness. And she didn't sleep. When *she* slept I did . . . My husband kept asking me to strip the walls and I couldn't do it. 'But why can't you?' he'd say and I'd point to the baby. 'Look at the size of her!' Then you feel guilty really because *why* is she controlling my life? . . . I think I resented all my time going to her really. Not so much boring as lonely. And frustrating. Both of those come into it. I think all the time I found that.
>
> (*Teacher, aged 30*)

Knowing that the period at home is a temporary phase makes many mothers better able to put up with it and, in some instances, marks the difference between not enjoying and enjoying the experience. The fact that they know they are not going to stay at home also makes it easier to confront and articulate its negative aspects.

> (*How did you feel about being at home full-time?*) Great! I have really enjoyed it. But I think it's possibly because I knew there was an end to it. I have a feeling that if I had finished work and wasn't going back to school that I'd be feeling restless perhaps. I've been feeling very guilty about letting things slide round the house though, thinking 'You've got nothing else to do – should be doing it sort of thing' . . . But I've got friendly with the neighbours. Before I wasn't really at home enough. Being able to go out and around the village everyday for walks and things. Just being able to waste time. And wander round the shops in the middle of the week . . . (*Have you felt able to make use of your abilities?*) Probably not, not really. But I'm finding new abilities and uses for my talents. (*Have you missed your job?*) Again, because I know I'm going back to it I'm not missing it desperately. But I know I'd be very sad if I knew I wasn't going back.
>
> (*Teacher, aged 37*)

> (*How do you feel about being at home full-time?*) I think because I know it's only a temporary thing I've enjoyed it . . . It's been nice not having to travel, being able to sit around in jeans all day. In some ways quite relaxing. But I haven't done things I intended to do . . . And some days have been fairly long. I found myself clock-watching for my husband to come home – especially on days when the baby has been irritable. There's always the feeling as soon as he comes through the door 'You have him'. I've tried not to do that. But I've quite enjoyed it. But if it hadn't been a temporary thing–.
>
> (*Local government administrator, aged 29*)

THINKING ABOUT THE RETURN

Given that so many women don't enjoy aspects of being at home it is not surprising that they also miss their jobs and look forward to going back to work. Four fifths of those going back to work miss their jobs, in particular the contact with other adults, compared with three fifths of mothers staying at home. But women who are about to return to their jobs are also anxious and worried about it. Two thirds express doubts and one quarter are very anxious indeed (see Table 3.2). This is not unexpected since the decision is principally the woman's alone and hence a very lonely decision, made with little discussion and support from other people (see Chapter 2). In addition the search for childcare and the decision to use a particular arrangement are largely the responsibility and task of mothers (see Chapter 4).

For many women, as their return draws nearer, so their anxieties increase. Some women eagerly seized upon the interview as an opportunity to pour out their worries and concerns. It is hard for mothers to find suitable people in whom to confide their doubts. Sources of advice and support normally open to women frequently prove inappropriate on this issue. Although a considerable number know other mothers who have gone back to work they are not necessarily people they know well. Indeed in some cases they have made their acquaintance for this very reason. Women are often reluctant to talk about their anxieties because they feel under considerable pressure to show that they can 'do it' – to prove themselves to bosses and work colleagues who think they will never manage the return, to sceptical and disapproving relatives and friends and, most of all, to themselves. Turning to others for reassurance or moral support involves exposing one's vulnerable side and, not surprisingly given the hostile climate, many women prefer to keep their worries to themselves.

> (*How do you feel about the prospect of going back to work?*) Pretty depressing. I think that's the only thing now that would get me down, if I stop to think about that Monday. (*And do you?*) Yes, now it's getting nearer and nearer ... Now it's getting quite prevalent. (*Has it been getting you down in the past months?*) Yes, but not to the extent that I'm showing it. But it's definitely been to the front of my mind. And if I didn't have that on the horizon I probably wouldn't get these lows at all. It's just if I stop and think that I'm going to have to leave for ... Most days it crosses my mind. I wouldn't say I go deep into thought about it ... But it's always there.
>
> (*Clerk, aged 23*)

Am I doing the right thing?

After five months at home, mothers are deeply attached to their babies and intimately concerned with their welfare. As the date of their return draws near mothers begin to ask themselves anew – ought I to be going back to work? The rightness or wrongness of the decision is considered in terms of its effects on the child. A question mothers commonly ask themselves is, 'Will the baby miss out if I'm not there?' The origin of these doubts lies in the dominant expectation that 'proper' mothers stay at home when their children are small. Even though three quarters of mothers going back to work don't necessarily agree with the idea that mothers collectively should stay at home they are none the less affected by the strength and prevalence of the idea and harbour doubts about their own individual situations and the effect on their own child (see Tables 3.3, 3.4).

> (*Have you had any doubts about your decision to go back to work?*) Yes. In the last couple of months before I went back. Because I'd got used to my routine at home, I'd got used to being with the baby and obviously I'd got quite a close relationship with him over that time. I wondered if I was doing

> the right thing – whether it was good for him, whether he'd be all right in the creche? Because I didn't know anything about that. And just physically how I'd be able to cope with it . . . Yes, it was a doubting time.
>
> (*Health administrator, aged 32*)

> The only time I feel miserable is when I contemplate going back to work. That's the only thing . . . I am trying to work out whether the reason I don't want to go back to work is purely because I was brought up – because it's traditional to have one parent at home with the child. And, therefore, I don't know whether I'm just feeling guilty because of that. Or whether actually intellectually I think it's not good to be in the hands of paid carers all week. I don't really know why I feel so bad about it . . . I can see it coming up on the horizon. It comes in waves.
>
> (*Language teacher, aged 31*)

Fear of separation and loss

A second and often related source of worry and anxiety occurs at the deep level of feelings rather than at the more surface level of values and beliefs. Mothers talk about 'handing the baby over to someone else'. In anticipating physical separation mothers fear that this may also lead to loss – of the child's affection or of influence over the child. Fear of losing the child is both real and symbolic. Mothers talk about finding substitutes for, rather than additions to, themselves as if the child could only be attached to one person. They don't even consider the effect of fathers' separation. The mother–child bond is seen as special and somehow akin to a monogamous relationship, such as marriage. This hampers women when they are about to leave their children in the care of other people. They often feel they are 'breaking the bond', 'abandoning' or 'leaving' the child. Liza has doubts both at the level of beliefs as well as feelings.

> I don't know if I'd say it was right. I don't think it's wrong. Difficult to be objective. I suppose *inside* myself I don't feel it's right. I feel I ought to be at home. But I've rationalised it to myself so much it's difficult to step back from that . . . I've always known I was going back to work . . . Originally I was going back in July. But as time approached I put it off and put it

> off. Then I suppose I thought 'I've got to go back.' I've tried to make the best arrangements for the baby that I can ... I've tried to work at all the positive things but ... I don't know. I suppose it's because he's so little and you're so attached to him. It's very very hard and the break is very hard. I suppose I feel that attached to him and he must feel that attached to me. It feels like you're abandoning him at a time when they need you.
>
> (*Librarian, aged 24*)

There are also some very real foundations to women's fears. One is that the baby may be ill-treated by the carer and be unable to say so or simply that he or she may be unhappy. Women fear that the carer won't look after the child as well as they themselves would. These fears are hardly surprising since mothers are continually told that they are the best people to bring up children. For five months mothers have been with their babies day and night with only very brief separations, although many mothers anticipate going back to work by leaving their children for short periods in the care of others. (They do so more frequently than mothers who expect to stay at home.) Mothers also worry that they themselves are going to both miss and miss out on the baby, that they won't be there to hear the first words or see the first steps.

> At the moment I could easily cry about it but I know it's because I don't want to leave her. I feel worse the nearer it gets. But on the other hand I don't want to lose my career and I don't want to lose my job. But I know this stage is over so quickly ... I worry about what I'm going to miss. I've told the nursery if she does anything at nursery I don't want to know. And when she does it with me I want it to be the first time.
>
> (*Teacher, aged 29*)

> Actually when the day came I didn't want to go back to work ... The main thing was handing him over to someone else. I was convinced nobody would understand him or look after him like I would ... Yes, I did have doubts. But it wasn't until I very nearly went back and he was coming up to four months and he was getting quite likeable that I felt I wanted to be with him a lot more.
>
> (*Radiographer, aged 26*)

Practical worries

A further cause for anxiety is the practicalities of managing and organising the return. Suddenly the day will dawn when the mother will wake up and have to get the baby and herself ready, take the child to the carer's and herself to work, usually with little help from anyone else. During the months at home women have got out of the way of getting up for work; now they have to manage with a baby as well. For some the very thought of it overwhelms them.

> I just don't know how easy it is going to be. I must admit when I am getting up twice in the night I don't see how I can do it. (*Does that worry you?*) It concerns me . . . I have some doubts. Will it work and can I make it work? Because some mornings it is at least 10 o'clock before I can even open the front door and walk out.
>
> (*Clerk, aged 35*)

Although the maternity rights legislation commits employers to keeping women's jobs open while they are on maternity leave they are only obliged to provide them with similar jobs when they return. If women are told they are going back to new jobs or new locations or simply don't know where they are going to be this can be an additional cause for concern. Even going back to the job you know can cause anxiety.

> I'm a bit apprehensive and very *rusty*, almost like the new girl.
>
> (*Telephonist, aged 30*)

Five months after the birth most mothers have made arrangements for their children's care but one in five of those using childminders has yet to do so (see Chapter 4). Indeed it is the explicit policy and practice of many social services departments who are responsible for putting mothers in touch with childminders *not* to hand out lists to mothers until they are within a month or two of returning to work. This practice causes considerable anxiety. Some women only feel able to make definite decisions about going back to work if their childcare arrangements have been finalised.

> I've been worried since I've had him, mainly about what he's going to be like when he's with the childminder. And whether I can get a childminder? I worry about the money situation now

> ... We tried to last on our savings but it's gradually going down and down all the time. I worry about that – whether we'll have enough to last us ... I worry because work is quite a distance away and that I won't be able to do the evening meetings when my husband's away overnight ... The worries are there all the time. I should imagine that's why I don't feel that good.
>
> (*Clerk, aged 23*)

Dealing with uncertainty

The articulation of doubt and anxiety may in itself help to make women's transition easier. Certainly if things don't run smoothly straightaway women aren't surprised or disappointed. Many try to anticipate the problems. Doubt and anxiety are responses to situations where people take risks and in going back to work there are a number of risks to be taken and uncertainties to be faced: there is no sure way to predict how it's going to work out. Ways of dealing with anxiety and worry vary. Some women prefer to give vent to their feelings; others endeavour to suppress them. One way of coming to terms with the prospect of going back to work is to tell yourself that you can always give it up if it doesn't work out.

> If my caring arrangements don't work out then I will stop work if he's unhappy. I'm sure he's going to be happier there than he is with me. But if not, I'd stop. I'm not having him shunted in a corner bored out of his mind.
>
> (*Careers officer, aged 30*)

'Seeing how it goes' is a further strategy: it parcels up time and reduces it to small manageable portions, especially when it appears to stretch ahead interminably.

Another way of dealing with uncertainty is to take a 'realistic' stance – expecting it to be difficult at the beginning. This may prove to be a good way of coping with present worries as well as preparing for the eventual return. Expecting it to be difficult may lead to preventative strategies.

> I think it's going to be tough until I get into any sort of routine. People say to me 'Have you got into a routine yet?' ... I haven't

> yet but I do feel I have to get into a routine when I go back to work. I've got to work that out now.
>
> (*Local government administrator, aged 31*)

Those who return to work early tell themselves that it is better for the child to be left before she or he becomes 'too attached'. None the less these mothers are aware of the general disapproval of 'leaving' young children in the care of anyone else.

> I decided to go back when he was three months because I read and was told that a baby gets more attached at about five to six months. I thought it would be harder for me and the baby to separate at that time. So I thought if I go at three months it will probably be easier to leave her ... I couldn't bear it if she cried when I left ... I still feel now 'Have I done anything to her?' by leaving her there ... I think I'll always feel guilty. I don't think I'll never not feel – that's because – I think everyone has got to be educated – because *they* always keep pointing it out. But there's not been any other model for these people to go by. She'll admire me – I keep thinking as I push her through the rain and snow. Someone's got to start the change!
>
> (*Teacher, aged 30*)

Feeling obligated

Even though the period just before the return is often filled with feelings of doubt, worry and anxiety, many women also feel they owe it to themselves and to others to go back to work. Over one half of mothers feel under an obligation to return with one fifth feeling torn in both directions and a further fifth who don't feel obligated at all. Women who intended to stay at home are much less bound by this feeling. Women who are going back to work are also much less likely to feel they have a choice about the matter than women who remain at home (see Tables 3.4, 3.5, 3.6, 3.7).

We take seriously and feel constrained by the wishes and opinions of people we respect or feel close to. The more powerful and salient the relationship the more constrained we may feel. But it is the *imagined* power of the other person as well as their actual power which determines how obligated we feel. Power does not have to be visible in order to exist nor does it have to be activated in order to exert itself. The ties which bind relationships are various; some are material, some social, some emotional, whilst many are experienced in more than one way. Women feel constrained by their husbands, their children, their employers and by themselves.

If their husbands have committed themselves to a view about their wives working, women appear to be greatly affected by their attitudes, even though they may not go so far as to describe themselves as feeling 'obligated'.

> I don't feel under obligation but I see his point of view, that it would bring more strain on the relationship and probably towards the baby. If we were short of money it would put additional strain on the marriage that probably it wouldn't take. (*You mean the family*?) Well, this is it. This is my husband's point of view. He doesn't want to sponge off other people. He wants to be able to have enough money to supply and provide for us ... (*Do you feel a duty then*?) Duty is a better word. I would feel I was letting him and the baby down if I didn't go back. I feel I'm letting her down by going back as well.
>
> (*Clerical worker, aged 23*)

In cases where the husband is in his second marriage and has to provide for the children of his first marriage the second wife may feel she has no choice but to resume work.

> Well, I feel a certain amount of obligation to my partner in as much as we could not have managed if I didn't. The additional pressure I would have brought to bear if I'd said 'I'm not going back to work' is that he would have had to reduce the maintenance. And he feels guilty enough about his son already without cutting back on the money. It was never said but I certainly *felt* it.
>
> (*Administrator, aged 31*)

Some women feel under an obligation to their employers and workmates especially if they have stated a clear intention to return. Where employers provide maternity pay in addition to the statutory minimum many women are bound to repay it if they don't go back. Women feel a strong sense of challenge to prove to their workmates and to the world that they can do it after all.

> Yes, I do feel if I don't go back I could just slowly wind down. I've spent six or seven hard years in employment. I feel a cosmic obligation to womankind, particularly to women at my firm because I said I was going back. I feel I owe it to other women who are going to have babies because it's rarely done there. People tend to leave. I only know of one other person who has gone back.
>
> (*Industrial journalist, aged 30*)

The sense of obligation towards the child is usually in the direction of not returning. Just over a fifth feel they owe it to the child not to go back with a mere four per cent feeling the opposite (see Table 3.6).

> I suppose I owe it to my child really – not to go back. I'm torn but part of me thinks I owe it to him to stay at home.
>
> (*Typing pool superintendent, aged 29*)

Those few who feel they ought to go back for their children's sake talk in terms of material provision.

> I owe it to him actually ... I said to myself if I didn't go back he would have to do without a lot of things. So I was going partly for him and partly for what we'd already got really. I mean I could quite easily have given up work and moved into a flat. That would have worked. It would have solved the problem. But then I thought 'Go back to work and have the things we've got already'.
>
> (*Radiographer, aged 26*)

People are bound by themselves as well as by what others think. Nearly one half of mothers feel they owe it to themselves to go back (see Table 3.7). Only a handful of women not returning feel the same way. A strong sense of self means placing positive value on what we are and what we do. Feeling that one owes it to oneself to continue working implies valuing one's occupational role. Not surprisingly women in professional and managerial jobs are particularly likely to feel an obligation to themselves to return. Women can feel obligated to themselves and to others at the same time.

> (*Did you feel in any sense that you owed it to anyone to go back to work?*) Yes, under an obligation to myself to see it through. It was a sort of personal commitment. Also to my husband because I thought it was only fair to give it a try and also to my workplace because I'd taken maternity leave and I'd felt in order to honour my contract I ought to go back.
>
> (*Hospital administrator, aged 32*)

Women's wishes

Many women have doubts or feel anxious about returning. Some feel constrained. But how many actually want to go back? Despite the doubts, worries and feeling of having to go back, the vast majority of women do want to, though over half would prefer part-time hours. In addition women want to cut down on travel and any 'extra hours' they are required to do after work. All this time is seen as time away from their babies.

> I think I'd probably just like to work some of the time and to be with the baby some of the time so he wouldn't have to be away for so long. Because it's quite a long time for him to be with a childminder – till the time we pick him up, especially if I have to do evening meetings at work and if my husband is working away overnight.
>
> (*Orders clerk, aged 23*)

Even given the choice, a quarter of women want to work full-time (see Table 3.8). Part-time hours involve considerable loss of benefits and pay. Some mothers cannot afford a drop in income nor do they think that being part-time is likely to mean less work in practice.

> If you are going to get up and go to work and organise it to that extent I think you might as well do it full-time and get the full benefit of it rather than try and do it part-time and get the worst of both worlds.
>
> (*Administrator, aged 31*)

> (*Would you prefer to return part-time?*) No. If my job had been different but having a half-term and a holiday every so many

weeks makes it acceptable. I don't think I'd be very happy working sort of week after week nine to five. I think that would be too much. But working shorter hours and longer holidays. Also my husband is off as well. It makes it a lot more acceptable.

(*Teacher, aged 31*)

CHAPTER 4

Finding childcare

> The decision was shared (with my husband), but I did all the finding of it. I decided to try and keep my options open. The first thing I did was to apply to the creche (at my workplace). I didn't get a place, but they gave me details of childcare in my (home area). The first thing I did was to look through the nurseries. The Council nurseries were out and there was only one private nursery. I went to Social Services about childminders and they said it was too early. I got in touch nearer the time, but they more or less said there's hardly anyone in this area who will take a baby. All you can do is just phone up the week before you're going back, which isn't very satisfactory . . . I had all the information there was, but it seems a very hit and miss affair . . . I thought Social Services were very off-hand. They said you haven't a chance of getting into a council nursery, which I knew, and they more or less said we'll give you a list of childminders, tell you who has got a vacancy and then it's up to you.
>
> (*Librarian, aged 34*)

WHO DOES THE WORK?

Women divide fairly evenly between those – just over half – who feel the job of arranging childcare is not inherently the mother's, but should be shared or done by whichever parent has most time and opportunity; and those – just under half – who feel it *should* be the mother's job. Most women in this second group feel that searching for childcare is their job because childcare is primarily their responsibility – 'you're the one who has to feel happy about leaving the baby' – and because the need arises 'because it's (the mother's) choice she's going back'. Some women also feel that mothers are more capable of finding good arrangements because they know the child better, and are better judges of other women.

> (It should be) the mother because she knows the child more than the father would do ... the mother is with her 24 hours a day. She has that instinct ... she would know instinctively if it was all right for her child to go to that person.
>
> (*Bank clerk, aged 24*)

Although half or more women do not believe that it should be the mother's job to find childcare, most arrangements are actually made mainly or wholly by mothers. In only a few cases are arrangements described as made by both parents together.

> I did this area (went to Social Services about childminders) and when I got no luck, he went to Social Services where he works, then he did all the phoning and we both went along to see the minder.
>
> (*Library assistant, aged 31*)

Rarest of all are arrangements made wholly or mainly by fathers.

> He got the nursery place because he works (for an employer who sponsors places at the nursery). He went and looked at the nursery and fixed it up.
>
> (*Polytechnic course administrator, aged 31*)

That childcare arrangements are so widely made by mothers may appear unsurprising – a taken-for-granted feature of life. Unsurprising it may be. Taken for granted it should not be, either on grounds of principle or practicality.

The timing of childcare arrangements may be determined by the mother's maternity leave: but the need for such arrangements arises because *both* parents are employed. Although fathers are out at work, this is no reason why the search for childcare should fall to mothers. Looking after a baby and home is as much work as paid employment and imposes its own constraints – having a young baby in tow does not make it easy to make enquiries and look at possible options. Even though they are out at work, most fathers could participate in the search for childcare in the evening or at weekends, or they could take a day or two's leave. Moreover, partly because of the limited options available, in the great majority of cases only one potential caregiver is visited at all before the arrangement is finalised.

In theory there is little or no practical reason why fathers cannot take joint responsibility but in practice mothers are left to assume the lead role. In this respect, the search for childcare is a microcosm of the division of childcare and other domestic tasks in dual earner households (see Chapter 9).

CONDUCTING THE SEARCH FOR CHILDCARE

A few women begin the search before they conceive; becoming pregnant may indeed be conditional on having arranged childcare.

> When we first decided to try for a child, I went down to Social Services to ask what were the possibilities, because we'd just moved into the area. When they discovered I wasn't a one parent family, they looked at me like someone who had got a fatal disease. Quite honestly they hadn't anything helpful to say ... I said I don't wish for (childcare) now, this is for 18 months time ... They said they couldn't prophecy if there would be any (childminders) free in 18 months (and) I certainly couldn't get into any kind of nursery because they are for single parent families ... Suffice to say, I got on with it myself. My husband went to the local church and briefly joined a group of tennis players and asked a woman there who asked around ... (the childminder found this way) seemed a very nice person ... she seemed competent and her children appeared well behaved ... *if I couldn't have found anyone, I certainly would not have become pregnant.*
>
> (*Teacher, aged 39*)

The most common time to begin looking for childcare is in the first six months of pregnancy. Most women – two-thirds – have begun before the birth, and nearly all of the remainder start in the first three months after the birth. However, a substantial minority – a third – have no definite arrangements by the time their baby is three months old, only a matter of weeks before resuming employment.

The timing involved is closely related to the type of care eventually used. If relatives are to become the carers, mothers usually make arrangements early: two-thirds start this search before they are six months pregnant and over half have their childcare tied up before their child is born. Most women who find a nursery place also start their search early – like women who use relatives, they often have a particular arrangement in mind from the start. Usually, though, they have to wait much longer to get their childcare settled: only about a quarter have a place arranged by the time their child is born and nearly half are still waiting for the confirmation of a nursery place when their baby is three months old.

The situation of women who use childminders is much the same when it comes to settling arrangements. Most have nothing finally arranged before the birth, and a large minority are still uncertain several months later. The main difference is that they are more likely to start looking later: half do not begin until after the birth.

Recommendations

Although publicly supported childcare is virtually unavailable, local authority Social Services departments do offer some assistance to parents searching for childcare. The extent and nature of this varies from authority to authority. Generally, though, they give parents only the most basic information, such as the names and addresses of the childminders and nurseries registered with the authority (as they are supposed to be by law).

Parents may also get assistance from health visitors. They often know about childminders and nurseries in their 'patch'. While Social Services departments are usually unwilling to comment on the quality of individual nurseries or childminders registered with them, health visitors are more likely to give an opinion or make a recommendation about local caregivers – though this again varies.

Very few parents rely solely on these services in their search for childcare. Far more, around half, depend entirely on informal sources of information and advice – relatives, friends and colleagues. Most women discuss childcare with at least one of these informal sources. Particularly valuable, though by no means generally available, is advice and support from other working mothers. They can offer their own experiences and provide information, understanding and reassurance. These are rarely available from husbands, relatives or the formal services.

Some parents, just under a half, consult both formal services and informal sources in their search for childcare. Sometimes they rely mainly on formal services, or consult both equally. On other occasions, formal services are used as a back-up or safety net, to be approached when arrangements made via informal sources fall through or if parents fear that such arrangements may fail to materialise. For instance, Social Services or health visitors are often asked about childminders in case an anticipated and preferred nursery place does not become available.

Relatives often offer to care for children without being asked: such unsolicited offers account for a third of the children who are cared for by relatives. Similarly, friends, friends of friends or even friends of relatives may offer their services as childminders. Except for a very small number found through advertisements, the remaining childminders come equally through formal services and informal sources. Nursery places are mostly found either because a parent knows of the nursery, because it provides for employees at his or her workplace, or through a work colleague who knows of one.

HOW WOMEN FEEL ABOUT THE SEARCH FOR CHILDCARE

Many mothers make arrangements without any contact with formal services. A third of those who do consult services describe them as unhelpful, far more than describe husbands, friends or relatives as unhelpful. Criticism of, and indeed contact with, services is far higher among women who use childminders or nurseries for their children. Women using relatives generally make arrangements more easily and have less need to consult formal services.

Some women who express dissatisfaction with formal services are not specific about what they would have liked from them. Instead they simply feel and say that there was insufficient support. The largest group with specific criticisms want better advice, for instance about childcare options and the quality of specific placements, or recommendations about specific childminders.

> I wish there had been somebody – Social Services or something – who could actually have things laid out, if someone had said, come and see me and discuss it . . . I spoke to the health visitors, but they weren't terribly helpful. They were trying to be but they didn't have any information. I thought they might be able to recommend a minder.
>
> (*Senior laboratory technician, aged 36*)

> I was given a long list (of childminders by Social Services) with the comment that 'of course there are several I wouldn't recommend – but I can't tell you who they are'.
>
> (*Senior accountancy assistant, aged 33*)

Two other main areas of complaint are made. Some women express a need for more information on what is available or information that is easier to find – 'You have to go looking for information, I don't think it's very accessible'. Others comment on the need for more childcare provision.

> You can't give information out about nothing. I think the State ought to provide a great part in seeing it is provided, even if it doesn't necessarily provide it itself. I think there needs to be a complete change of attitude, so workplaces see their staff as family people as well. If they are going to train women who have (also) trained outside, and see them go for lack of decent childcare facilities – I think it's terrible . . . but we haven't got a voice. How many women are there in Parliament?
>
> (*Local authority administrator, aged 31*)

Only a few women describe making childcare arrangements as 'hard' or 'harder than expected'. A similar small number say it was 'easy', as they expected. The largest group however – two thirds – describe it as 'easier than expected'. This reflects a common anticipation that it will be difficult to find somewhere, except perhaps after 'trailing around' many places.

> I thought it would be a long drawn out affair and the day I'm due back at work (I'd) still not have anywhere . . . at least eight girls (at work) had had awful problems.
>
> (*Library assistant, aged 25*)

Having a choice

But, when women's apparent satisfaction with the search for childcare is judged against two basic criteria – that those who want it should have some choice of childcare open to them and that parents should be able to make arrangements at roughly the time that they prefer – the situation is less satisfactory.

For some women, having a choice of care is irrelevant. From the start, they only consider one arrangement acceptable and are able to make such an arrangement. In most of these cases, the only acceptable carer is a relative, who often offers her services without needing to be asked. Sometimes the decision to return to work depends on a particular carer being ready and willing to have the child.

> I talked about it (with my mother) before the pregnancy. But I finalised it when I was pregnant ... unless I'd had something like that on the horizon, I don't think I'd have gone ahead and got pregnant. It was a sort of unspoken arrangement. She said on several occasions, if I had a baby and went back to work, she'd have it for me. I'd never consider anything else. It had to be family. I could not leave her with a stranger. It was easier than I'd expected.
>
> (*Clerical worker in civil service, aged 23*)

Others mothers do not have such clear-cut preferences at the start, but receive offers of childcare which, once made, seem so suitable that they preclude the need to look for or consider further options. Again the issue of choice is, for them, irrelevant.

> (My friend and I) went out together for a drink, about a week before the birth. She said she was fed up with her job and 'What are you going to do with the baby?' and I said 'Get a childminder' and she said 'I'll have it'. I said 'Great. But we'll leave it open until I've had it' and I just wandered over there one afternoon and she said 'When do you want me to start?' ... it was much easier than I'd expected, it was all sorted out in 10 minutes.
>
> (*Education welfare officer, aged 29*)

For a third group of women, the issue of choice is relevant. There is no obviously right arrangement available, and they feel they can choose between types of childcare. Normally this choice is narrow, restricted to two types – for instance a relative and a childminder, or a nursery and a childminder.

> There's a creche over in one of the schools where my husband works. As soon as I was pregnant, we got her name down for that ... (my employer is) also due to open a creche and when they opened a list, I put her name down for that. Only later, my husband's sister suggested that my sister-in-law might like to look after her ... I could have got a place (in the creche, but) I think it's better on the whole to have personalised individual care. It just seemed the best way. Also it's convenient being so close to us ... it was easier than I'd expected.
>
> (*Local government solicitor, aged 29*)

> First of all (my husband and I) talked about what the options appeared to be – a childminder or something. We thought we'd have to employ a childminder. Then my husband found out (from a friend) at school that they (friend and his partner) had made an enquiry at a creche. Then we went along and had a look and put our names down.
>
> (*Teacher in language school, aged 31*)

Just under half the women are satisfied with the degree of choice: they either feel choice is irrelevant or feel they have some choice between types of childcare *and* in addition are satisfied with the timing involved in making the childcare arrangement. Women who use relatives are twice as likely to be in this group – with choice and timing satisfactory – than are women who use nurseries or childminders.

Around half the mothers feel they have no choice between different types of childcare. For some, as just described, this is irrelevant; they feel no need for choice. They may even have some choice available on paper – between, for instance, their mother or some other relative and a childminder – but don't feel themselves to have a choice, since no-one but their chosen carer is acceptable.

However, most of the women who feel they have no choice are not committed to one particular carer. This group includes women who have literally no alternatives available; and also some women who may seem to have a choice, but consider that the alternative on offer is unacceptable.

> A friend offered. I didn't like her actually. She was prepared to have Gill, but she's on the seventh floor of a block of flats and I couldn't see her getting out.
>
> (*Teacher, aged* 29)

Most mothers who arrange care with a relative or at a nursery know that childminding is available if all else fails. By contrast, most women who use childminders have no other type of care available; they are least likely to feel there are other types of care open to them. They may however have a choice between different childminders (even though most do not actually visit more than one before making an arrangement). Women who use relatives and nurseries usually don't feel they have any choice between different relatives or between different nurseries. So, although most women feel they have a choice either between types or within a type, few have both.

Some women would prefer to start their search for childcare or to settle matters earlier. Delays occur for several reasons. Nurseries may only offer a place well after the child is born, sometimes at the very last minute; offers of places depend on vacancies coming up and this is frequently unpredictable. Women planning to use childminders who want to make arrangements well in advance can run up against Social Services departments whose policy it is not to give out information about childminders until a few weeks before parents need a place. These departments argue that childminders will not or cannot reserve places too far in advance. Finally, some women find themselves looking for childcare at the last minute when arrangements made earlier fall through.

Six mothers

About half of the women experienced lack of choice or were dissatisfied with the timing of their search for childcare, or both. The six cases that follow are taken from this group. They illustrate some of the reasons for lack of choice or for unsatisfactory timing, as well as some of the dilemmas that these difficulties can produce.

ROSEMARY

A 25 year old clerical officer in the civil service, Rosemary has been married for two years to a painter and decorator. She moved to London from the north-east 3 years ago. Her parents and other relatives still live in the north-east. Rosemary has few friends in London. Like a number of women she looked into the possibility of a nursery place, only to find none are available – 'I enquired about nurseries but they only took children over two'. She also approached Social Services.

> I phoned the Social Services up. (Childcare) was one thing I was worried about. (I rang) just after I was pregnant. They said phone six to eight weeks before I wanted to go back to work. I phoned up before Christmas (when the child was six weeks old). They said they'd ring back. I expected them to ring back straight after Christmas, but it was a good deal later when I'd already arranged something. My health visitor knew I was wanting a childminder and she mentioned (this childminder) to me. She had seen this woman and she's known her for a time and she happened to meet her in the street and she mentioned she was looking for another child. I'd have preferred to start earlier, I think it would have put my mind more at ease . . . If I'd had a choice, I'd have had my Mam or Dad.

MARY

A 28 year old secretary in a bank, Mary has been married for two years to a laboratory technician. Her mother is dead and she has only a small circle of relatives and friends, none of whom are frequently seen. Mary's situation is made harder by her employer leaving it until the last minute to tell her where she will be sent when she resumes work.

> My husband's sister offered to look after her and I didn't think it was a very good idea on the social side. To go over there for a visit and my little girl wouldn't know whose mum it was and who to take notice of . . . I made enquiries of Social Services even before she was born. They gave me six names and addresses. I phoned a couple, but they were quite a way away.

It's really a case that I don't know where they (the bank who employ her) are going to send me.

I had phoned up nurseries and they'd told me it was out of the question. I was four months pregnant and wanted to get things sorted out. I was disappointed. They asked 'Are you a one parent family?' It didn't seem fair, I know someone at work who'd got her little girl into a nursery and she didn't get married until her daughter was five, although she was living with the father. I have got a childminder hopefully arranged. I arranged it when Jean was five weeks, and (the childminder) said she'd phone if she didn't have a vacancy by the time I went back. She's a newly registered one. No-one really knows much about her so I'm a little bit frightened about that. As soon as I hear from the bank, and get a definite date (to resume work), I'll phone up and check it. [In fact, this childminder 'fell through', and Mary found a new childminder from the Social Services list.]

LORRAINE

A 28 year old ward sister, Lorraine has been married for four years to a self-employed builder. Nearly all her family live in Ireland, so that her 'ideal' choice of care – a relative – is, as in Rosemary's case, not feasible. Lorraine's situation is complicated by her shiftwork, which many childminders are not prepared to consider. In the end, she made an arrangement with a childminder, with her husband providing back-up.

It was arranged *before* I went on maternity leave. An auxiliary at the hospital was stopping work. She has her own child. I knew of her and she volunteered. I kept in touch and went round with Andrew. All was fixed. Then her husband got promoted, which involved bringing clients home – a baby was not a suitable mix. She dropped out and I had 10 days to find a new arrangement. I got the names of three childminders from the clinic and visited them all (and made a new arrangement). I rang others, but they were not interested in weekend work [needed because of shiftwork]. There was no choice. (My hospital) has no nursery and a nanny was too expensive. I'd ideally like a relative, someone I know, or a nursery.

JEAN

A 24 year old personal assistant/secretary in a bank, Jean has been married for four years to a lorry driver. She has a more extensive network of friends than Mary, but most of her family live 60 miles away in the Midlands, including her mother who is her 'ideal' choice. Jean's situation is further complicated because she lives in a small village in the country where there are no registered childminders. Jean eventually decided to accept her mother-in-law's offer of care.

> She (husband's mother) offered . . . we were around there and I said I'd probably have to go back to work and she said 'I'll have Carol' . . . my sister-in-law also offered but I kept looking at her children and wondered if I really wanted her to be like them . . . I did ask the health visitor if any people round here were childminders (but) there aren't any.
>
> The ideal would be to have a creche or a trained minder (or) if my mum was nearer, she'd be ideal. I think she wouldn't get so involved because she's still got my little brother at home, so she has other people to think about.

JANET

A 21 year old assistant supervisor in a bank, Janet married a self-employed motor mechanic shortly before her daughter's birth. She has a large circle of friends and relatives. Unlike the others, but like some mothers who do use relatives, she faces pressures about which relative should provide care; these pressures cut her off from some choices that, in theory, are available to her and push her towards an unwelcome arrangement.

> I started by thinking of a childminder . . . (but) it was decided that my mother-in-law would have him. My husband always originally wanted his mother to have Peter. I was the one who was debating because I felt it was unfair one parent should have her when the other didn't. I felt there'd be fights. So I was going to have the childminder to keep the two separate, not to squabble over him. But I was sort of brought to my senses over it. His mother won't want any money for it, which helps, and a childminder would be a strange person, out of the family. We

worked it out, it would be better for him to be with someone he knows already.

My husband wasn't really helpful because I was against what he wanted in the first place. It was difficult to talk because he was adamant that was what he wanted. He didn't want to discuss it and it took a little time before he would.

My ideal would be a creche (or I'd) still opt for a childminder or if my mother wasn't working, I'd prefer her or my grandma ... As far as my husband is concerned, it's the best thing for the child. I still have my doubts in the back of my mind.

ALISON

A 32 year old joint head of year at a comprehensive school, Alison has been married for 13 years to another teacher. Her own family live in Birmingham, and are unavailable except to provide temporary care while a more permanent arrangement is made. She is unusual in having access to a creche provided for teachers in the local authority where she is employed.

> I had experience of visiting the creche over a period of six years, so I knew them intimately. I knew the two women who work there very well. Before I was pregnant, (I decided) if I had a baby, that's where I'd go. I did consider if I didn't get in, what the next step would be ... that's where the problems really started, that's where I began thinking, 'If it comes to it, I'm just going to extend my maternity leave unpaid' ... I imagine it would have been a childminder. I have no relations nearby. I don't think I'd have been very happy at all. That would have been a big problem. I don't know what I would have done. It had even got to the stage where my mother was going to come down and live with us in the week.

The nursery eventually offered a place when her child was three and a half months old.

> (I'd have liked it) much earlier, but they simply didn't have a place. Someone left and it was a matter of who on the list got the place. (*It was very close to your return to work?*) Oh yes. (*There was a possibility you wouldn't return when the new*

> *term began*?) Yes. I was saying 'I won't go back until I find somewhere suitable' . . . if the worst had come to the worst, and I found that financially I had to go back (before I got the creche place) I could have taken her to a friend – (but that was) a very vague possibility in that she lives (in another borough) and I don't have a car.

'Ideal' childcare

For many women – roughly half – the childcare arrangement finally made does not coincide with the childcare they say they would 'ideally' choose. This overall figure conceals considerable differences. Two thirds of the women with a place at a nursery and just over half the women who use a relative feel that what they have got is 'ideal'. Among women who use a childminder, only a third are similarly satisfied.

Where the ideal does not coincide with what has been arranged, most women want a different type of childcare altogether. Nurseries – and especially workplace nurseries – are most popular. Childminding, the most common actual arrangement, is much less popular. Moreover, women who give childminding as their ideal include some who specify that they want childminding by a friend or to share a nanny with another mother. A fourth type of childcare – nannies – gains considerable support (see Table 4.1).

A few whose ideal differs from what they actually arrange, want the same type of childcare, but a different person or nursery.

> I'd prefer a (particular) friend to have him (rather than the childminder arranged) . . . (my friend) is that much older and she's got similar views to what I have about taking care of them.
>
> (*Clerical officer in civil service, aged 23*)

Nursery users are most likely to want such a change, usually because their ideal would be a nursery closer to home or with more staff.

> (I'd choose) the same sort of nursery she's in now, with one or two more staff, so there would be more staff . . . and longer hours and nearer home.
>
> (*Teacher, aged 25*)

These preferences need treating with caution. Answers to hypothetical questions of the 'What would you choose in an ideal world?' variety are notoriously unreliable guides to what people do in practice – especially when people are asked to consider options which are not generally available.

The case of nurseries illustrates the point. Nursery provision is scarce in Britain, particularly for children in the age group we are considering here. Much of what does exist is under-resourced, isolated and neglected; the whole area has been largely ignored since 1945. Given this context, it is surprising that nurseries attract as much interest and support as they do. Wider availability of adequately funded, good quality nursery care, supported as an acceptable childcare option, might well increase still further the already high number of parents attracted to this type of care. Certainly the demand for and use of nurseries for children under three years in Denmark (see Chapter 1) supports such a conclusion.

The results of asking women in present circumstances what childcare they would ideally like do not provide a sound basis for prediction and planning. Nevertheless, they are of some value and interest in considering the future of childcare services. They suggest that several different sorts of childcare appeal to parents – or at least mothers – and that many are attracted to options, such as nurseries or nannies, that at present are available only to a few families.

This diversity of views also reflects diversity in the qualities that are valued and sought in childcare. In explaining why they would choose a particular type of childcare women give a wide range of reasons. Those using nurseries emphasise the value they attach to their children being with and in a group of children, and the importance of having 'professionally trained' staff, proper supervision and good facilities. Some also are concerned to avoid their child developing too close a relationship with one other adult which might threaten their own relationship. The importance of having their children cared for close to where they work is emphasised by some women who use workplace nurseries.

> I feel I'd mind the baby having a relationship with one other woman ... at the creche he prefers certain women but it doesn't bother me because there are so many ... he'll never sort of have a special relationship ... I'm jealous, I want my own to want me.
>
> (*Theatre nurse, aged 29*)

> The number of children and their age range makes (the nursery) more what I want for him . . . a minder can be a bit restrictive.
>
> (*Teacher, aged 30*)

> I like the idea of a nursery because there's a lot of peer pressure on staff. Everyone has to be seen to be doing their job well, (and) I'm sure people working in a nursery are more interested in their work than a childminder.
>
> (*College administrator, aged 31*)

> I felt being so young, she needs to be as near me as possible . . . I couldn't concentrate going off to work, knowing she was here (in home village, 40 miles from London).
>
> (*Senior laboratory technician, aged 32*)

Women using relatives or childminders attach more importance to personal or individual attention, and often want their child to have a close, one-to-one relationship with the caregiver.

> I think I would have been able to find a nursery, but I wanted him to be looked after by one person who could love him and give him a lot of attention.
>
> (*Teacher, aged 30*)

> I wouldn't be happy with any form of group care because I want her to have as near a one-to-one relationship as she has with me.
>
> (*Senior laboratory technician, aged 32*)

Women using relatives, and occasionally friends, think it is important for the child to be cared for by someone they know and trust, and consider a 'stranger' unacceptable.

> It's safer because I know her. He'll get the special care he needs with my mother and I can talk to her about what he's been doing.
>
> (*Civil servant, aged 24*)

> It's someone who cares for her as opposed to doing it for a job, (my mother) knows me and John's needs and she's somebody close.
>
> (*Nursery nurse, aged 25*)

Nannies were seen as an attractive proposition by some women who attached importance to the child being cared for in the home, for the child's sake and sometimes the mother's.

> I don't think he gets as much attention (at a childminder) or the same kind of care or probably as much as a nanny would ... (being at a childminder) means he's not in his own home, that's a minus ... he's not so used to this place ... and the thing about a childminder is at the end of the day I have to come home, clean everything up, do the nappies, get all the shopping. A nanny would do all of it.
>
> (*Environmental housing officer, aged 28*)

> I'd probably like to have a nanny who came to the house and looked after him in familiar surroundings.
>
> (*Teacher, aged 31*)

The values attached by mothers to different qualities and characteristics in childcare arrangements are no more immutable than their views on ideal types of childcare. In different circumstances, different values might be emphasised. As with ideal childcare, the point to be made is that there is not, and is unlikely to be, uniformity in what mothers want from and value in childcare. This diversity needs to be recognised and taken into account in any consideration of how childcare provision might or should be made.

CHAPTER 5

Back to work

> I think it is the mum's choice to go back to work or not. And I think if they are going to get a job they should do the job as good as the next person. And if they can't they shouldn't be working.
>
> (*Teacher, aged 31*)

DIFFICULTIES THAT WOMEN FACE

Mothers going back to work after childbirth are often hard on themselves. But employers are very hard on mothers. There are virtually no concessions for working mothers or working fathers with young children. The only requirement made of employers is to give women their jobs back or to find them similar work if their former jobs are no longer available. Not only do women have to cope with the sudden separation from their children, they are thrust back into their jobs with little or no support to cushion the experience. There are no training programes to help them catch up on changes that have taken place in their absence. They are not entitled to work shorter hours in the first weeks which would enable them to ease themselves into their jobs and their children into daycare gradually. Employers are not obliged to offer part-time work or job sharing for those who would like to cut down on their hours permanently. Most distressing of all for mothers is the fact that if their children are ill they are not officially entitled to take time off.

Consequently mothers must work under similar conditions to women without children. Officially and often unofficially they are treated no differently. Mothers' experiences at work hinge on the dispositions of their superiors and colleagues: they are reliant on their goodwill, encouragement and unofficial favours, and must manage as best they can.

Women who leave

Almost all women who intend five months after childbirth to go back to work at the end of maternity leave do so. However, by the time their child is 11 months old, a handful (14 women) do give up. Many mention several reasons for their decision although some always intended to return only for a brief period in order to repay their maternity pay – a condition required by employers who provide some maternity pay over and above the statutory minimum.

A local government officer decided to resign for the specific reason that her husband had a new job which meant they had to move away from London. She also mentions other subsidiary factors which clearly helped her come to terms with leaving work: the feeling of not being able to cope and the lack of support at work and at home.

One woman resigned after four weeks. This was mainly because of lack of support, especially at work.

> I couldn't cope with the journey, travelling, doing my work properly, coming home here and keeping the house in order. It was all too much. It was all right for the first couple of weeks. It was something new. But after that . . . I was getting very run down. I felt I had no time. I was getting so tired I couldn't do anything. Also I found people at work – their attitude – 'You're not going to get any favouritism because you've got a baby. It isn't an illness'. I said 'I don't expect any favouritism' . . . If the Inland Revenue had allowed me to change to a local office I could have carried on. It was a big relief to give up. I don't think the baby suffered at all but he might have in the long term. I'm glad to have given it a try. But I'm also relieved to have given it up.
>
> (*Taxation officer, aged 22*)

GREAT EXPECTATIONS?

Because there are no official employment practices designed to support them, women have low expectations of their employers. They do not expect them to take account of what they regard to be their 'private' responsibilities and the majority do not consider the issue at all in terms of fathers' work patterns or commitment to their children. Even so, asked directly about what employers *ought* to provide, most mention something: half mention childcare facilities, a third say time off for children's illness and less than one fifth suggest 'flexible hours' (see Table 5.1). In talking about their experiences as working mothers many women feel somewhat ambivalent. Given the absence of provision and the lack of public debate on the opportunities and conditions for combining work and parenthood when children are young this is perhaps hardly surprising.

Low expectations emerge over a number of issues. Some women regard concessions as 'soft options'. 'If you work full-time you have to accept that you work the same as everybody else and you shouldn't be entitled to special privileges – time off and things like that'. Yet, at the same time, women clearly take for granted concessions which over the years have been wrung from employers by the trade unions – time off for breaks, lunch hours and holidays. Some women echo their employers' concern with efficiency and profit. 'They've got businesses to run haven't they? And businesses don't run on sentimentality'. Good employment practices can thereby be dismissed as costly and sentimental. Possible benefits to employers in terms of improving the motivation and stability of the workforce are not mentioned.

Women's 'gratitude' for even very small concessions, including those which employers are legally obliged to provide, such as time off for medical checks in pregnancy, is a further indicator of low expectations. A woman is 'grateful' for being allowed an extra half hour on her lunch break to take her child for a hearing test. Another is 'grateful' for a job share even though it means demotion and being put on a pay grade she had left years ago.

Low expectations are also reflected in women's zealousness to be seen as reliable and hardworking when they get back to work. Many say that they are reluctant to take time off even for their own illnesses. In fact, women also take little leave for their children, often making other arrangements. There are very real grounds for their fears about taking time off. One is the stereotyped label of 'unreliable worker' which is frequently attached to mothers who go out to work. Women are concerned that any preferential treatment of working mothers might exacerbate already existing discrimination against women in the workplace.

> I've never needed to get off early. I've always made sure that the baby doesn't get in the way of work. That's the first thing they look for . . . I won't give them the chance . . . My boss was quite surprised that I don't talk about the baby at work . . . When I'm at work I've got to be efficient in my job . . .
>
> (*Bank clerk, aged 22*)

Women are therefore reluctant to ask for concessions. By carrying out their jobs even more efficiently than before they avoid being stigmatised.

The other ground for concern is the uncertain economic climate – the fear of cuts and unemployment which pervades many sectors of employment at present.

> Sometimes I am reluctant to take time off that's owing to me. The reason I don't is the abolition of the GLC. It's a bit dodgy at the moment . . . There are a lot of extra responsibilities and they're trying not to take on extra staff.
>
> (*Local government worker, aged 31*)

EMPLOYMENT PRACTICES

Asked directly which official practices and policies they have found helpful as working parents, few can think of any (see Table 5.1). Employment issues which are likely to affect women's return include maternity rights and the way they are handled, whether women return to the same job, the availability of part-time work, job sharing and time off.

How do maternity rights help?

Women's attitudes to maternity rights, like their attitudes to employers' treatment of working parents generally, are fairly unquestioning of the status quo. On the whole, women's knowledge about maternity rights tends to be limited to their own experiences. In many cases this information has not been easy to come by. Most obtain information through personnel departments, colleagues or government leaflets and information from Citizens' Advice Bureaux. Women do not usually expect more than the statutory minimum and only express criticism if their employers are actively unhelpful, as some are. For example, some employers refuse to grant women their maternity pay until after their return to work.

Giving notice of the intention to take maternity leave and to return to work are important ways in which women keep their options open, even if they do not ultimately expect to return. These rights protect women from unfair dismissal and, should anything go wrong at the birth, ensure that they have a job to return to. They are however of little practical help in enabling women to go back to work, especially since they are not backed up with any public childcare provision.

Britain is virtually unique in Europe in leaving it to women's discretion whether or not to re-enter employment in the first weeks after childbirth. This is probably because there is such a strong belief that women ought not to work at all in the early years of a child's life. It seems that where a matter is entirely taken for granted a law is not required. Most European countries impose a ban on women working for several weeks which they see as essential to the health and well-being of women and their babies.

In Britain the statutory maternity leave period is rarely taken in full. On average British women go back to work five months after the birth. A major reason for the early return is that so little of the leave period is paid. Many of the early returners, especially those in poorly paid jobs, do so because of financial pressures. Another reason is that babies are less likely to be 'clingy' at this age than later which makes the transition to daycare easier. The option of a longer leave period is therefore unlikely to encourage more women to take up their maternity rights unless the paid part is also substantially increased.

Nationally there have been very few cases of litigation where employers have tried to prevent women entitled to do so from returning to work. All but three women in the study were reinstated in their former or similar jobs after their return. None of the three brought cases against their employers, although in two cases the employers clearly did not comply with the law. In the third, the woman's job disappeared in the reorganisation of the Health

Service, a situation specifically excluded from protection by the Act.

SANDRA

When Sandra returned from maternity leave to her post as an administrator in a small video company she found she had been replaced. She always intended to resume work (by law women are not required to confirm their intention until after the birth) and within the required period wrote to her boss stating her intention to return. Since he didn't reply she went to see him. He offered her two choices: a lump sum of money (£3,000) in lieu of her job or a lower paid secretarial post (previously she had been on £10,000 a year). Sandra was stunned and went to the CAB for advice. They advised her to bring a case against the firm for 'unfair dismissal'. She decided that it wasn't worth 'all the hassle'. In all probability she would not get her job back and instead would be awarded a sum of money by the tribunal as compensation, likely to be similar to the amount offered by the company. Also, going to an industrial tribunal is a long-drawn-out process which she did not relish. Instead she took the company's offer and eventually found a new job as a 'temp' on a much reduced wage.

Will I get the same job back?

The statutory rules require employers to reinstate women in the same or 'substantially similar work' on their return to work. Most do go back to their former jobs. But nearly a third experience some changes in their work situations. The most common experience was a move sideways to a new section or department. These moves often involved a change of duties or area of work. A number of women, mostly bank clerks, were transferred to another branch of the organisation. Government departments and large firms can more easily arrange transfers than small organisations: for example, a counter clerk at the Department of Employment was transferred to an office nearer home which helped her considerably. Most of these changes are initiated by employers and not by the women.

Most (under two thirds) accept the changes but over a third are unhappy. A bank clerk returned to find she had been moved to another building. She found the change 'quite taxing' but quickly became reconciled – 'I'm lucky to have a job'. Some women welcome a transfer if it means being nearer their child's carer and/or their home. Long journeys threaten to overwhelm women especially when they have to take their children with them on public transport.

A handful of women on maternity leave seek a total change of job, looking for work that fits in more easily with their new roles as mothers. This usually means changing employers. For example, a psychiatric nurse, responsible for 'down and outs' in hostels in central London, decided that her job was incompatible with motherhood and applied for a job as a nursing officer in the health district near her home, which was more convenient geographically and less demanding emotionally.

Seven of the women experienced a job change involving demotion and the same number were promoted after their return. As already indicated in Chapter 1, women aren't entitled to be considered for promotion whilst on maternity leave. Once back at work if they think they are being discriminated against in the promotion stakes, for example, their only legal recourse is to the Sex Discrimination Act. Such discrimination is notoriously difficult to prove under the present construction of the law. A junior school teacher returned from maternity leave and told the Head that she wanted to apply for a more senior post that had become available in the school.

> The Head made it clear that I was not going to get it. He thinks I'm not going to be there much longer. I'm irritated beyond belief ... He doesn't think I'll be able to do out of school activities ... He said 'You're such a good mother. I *know* you'll want to be with your daughter *all* the time'.
>
> (*Teacher, aged 28*)

Can I work shorter hours?

When women return from maternity leave the statutory rules oblige them to return full-time. Very few women go back on a part-time basis since they have no legal entitlement. Some, but again only a tiny minority, manage to negotiate part-time hours shortly after their return. Women's reasons for wanting to do so include wanting to see more of their children and feeling burdened by combining full-time work with childcare responsibilities.

Six months after her return a 36 year old planning assistant reduced her hours by working a three day week. Her mother, who looks after her baby, was beginning to find her 'a bit of a handful' especially since she now slept very little during the day. 'My employer was very understanding about me going part-time.'

Another woman was less fortunate. She found the long journey on public transport to her husband's aunt who looks after the child very tiring and she asked her employer if she could work part-time. She was offered, and unwillingly accepted, a lower paid job as a waitress. She is now able to work a shorter day and a four day week.

> I found it all too much on the very first day so I asked if I could go part-time . . . I enjoyed my old job. I don't like this one at all . . . But it's better now I'm part-time. By the time I got the baby to his aunt's and got back again most of the day was gone.
>
> (*Trainee cook, aged 20*)

One half of women say they would like to work shorter hours, at least to start with. However, the conditions under which employers are prepared to offer part-time work are often poor. Whilst on maternity leave a teacher in a language school decided that she wanted to return part-time. At first her boss seemed ready to negotiate.

> I was really surprised. I started off like you do when you bargain – with what I wanted but I was prepared to go down. In the end I offered everything except 45 minutes a week teaching and he said that wasn't possible. Then he offered me 3 days a week but only temporary. And he said that if I went part-time for a couple of months then I didn't have the automatic right to go back to full-time work afterwards. So I wasn't guaranteed my job back.
>
> (*Language school teacher, aged 31*)

The change to shorter hours entails becoming a part-time worker with the associated loss of status, benefits and a lower rate for the job. Those who work less than 16 hours a week have to have been with the same employer for five years to benefit from employment protection rights covering unfair dismissal, redundancy and maternity leave (those who work less than eight hours a week have no protection at all). At present, the government is trying to raise the 16 hour threshold to 20, which would exclude many job sharers from these important employment rights (it also wants to raise the eight hour threshold to 12). The prospect of these losses may well deter women from trying to negotiate part-time hours, especially as they feel financially responsible for the costs of childcare. This is especially true if childcare fees do not fall by the same proportion as their wages: childminders charge such low fees that they may be unwilling to cut their already very low incomes when the mother reduces the child's hours.

None the less over half the women would like shorter hours if only as a *temporary* measure, especially in the first weeks when they are getting used to working again and settling their children in with their new carers. In only a few instances do 'lenient' bosses grant women a permanent or temporary option of shorter hours. Most who request the change are unsuccessful.

> One thing that got me annoyed when I first came back to work. I wanted to work shorter hours to begin with ... I was willing to discuss it with my boss but she wouldn't even give me a time in her diary to come and talk about it. But I went and she wouldn't let me. Now she's doing shorter hours after she's been off ill for several months!
>
> (*Local government administrator, aged 30*)

As well as providing an adjustment period shorter hours can offer a solution to difficulties, for example children who take time to settle with the carers. A nurse returned to work for financial reasons when her child was 14 weeks old, but the baby refused to take the bottle. The woman was in 'quite a state' but her boss was not sympathetic – 'They thought I was worrying too much.' Eventually she was grudgingly allowed *slightly* shorter hours but only on a temporary basis. This caused so much envy and animosity among her nursing colleagues that, after six months, she gave up the struggle and resigned.

Is job sharing a solution?

Although job sharing is part-time or rather half-time, it is quite different from part-time employment. Job sharers are currently granted the same pay and conditions as full-timers but on a pro rata basis. Job sharing is therefore a useful option for women who wish to maintain all their employment benefits and to keep their place on the career ladder. They must however be able to afford a substantial reduction in earnings.

Few women know very much about the practicalities of job sharing or whether it is an option at their place of work. Even so, nearly one half (a similar proportion to those preferring shorter hours) say they would like to consider it. Women who want to job share often meet with resistance even when it is supposed to be available. A library assistant who works for one of the 'progressive' local authorities found someone with whom to share her job. Yet both became part-timers because of the intransigence of the authority's library division.

Large organisations which have many workers in similar types of work would find job sharing relatively simple to organise. However, many large employers, notably the NHS and some private firms, are reported as being ill-disposed to the practice. An executive officer in the Inland Revenue comments that job sharing in her department is not aimed at working mothers. 'Part-time work is for people over 55. Job splitting is not for working mothers – only for unemployed people to be trained or taken on.'

Problems with unsocial hours

Women who have to collect children from their carers, as most do, need to leave on time at the end of the day. If meetings are organised after work, especially at the last moment, this can make life very difficult. An administrator in a large multi-national company in central London works 15 miles away from home and the private nursery which she uses for her child. She does most of the 'ferrying' because her husband is rarely available.

> I can never stay after 4.30 at work because the nursery closes at 5.30 . . . I can barely put in the hours, let alone the extra hours. This is awkward because I used to work *all* hours. Also I belong to a professional association and all the meetings start at 4.30. That has been a real disadvantage in that I haven't been visible.
>
> (*Administrator, aged 31*)

After several months of struggle and pressure from her husband she resigned and started looking for a more convenient job nearer home.

A clerk in a graphics firm is under pressure to stay on at work at the end of the day. But she has to leave in order to collect her child from the childminder.

> At 5.30 I have to go and you get people saying 'Could you please do this for me before you go?' That used to affect me. People are beginning to forget I've got a child. They take it for granted that I'm going to stay on and help them out. It's very difficult when you are put in a job with that responsibility and have to say 'I can't stop now.' And what would the Managing Director say if people complained that I just left them hanging. That puts a lot of pressure on you. I've got to go home but, on the other hand, I think it's my responsibility to help them
> (*Orders clerk, aged 23*)

Some jobs include compulsory 'out of hours' work, such as evening work or weekends on call, as distinct from optional overtime. Women frequently want to avoid this, especially in the early weeks back at work. Again relaxation of these demands has to be informally negotiated with bosses and colleagues. Women are forced to rely on individuals' sympathy and generosity. A senior medical officer is 'allowed' to opt out of being on call every 10 days. (She is of course not paid for this duty.) But opting out can be difficult since it upsets the 'give and take' between workmates. Moreover some organisations like the Health Service depend upon people 'volunteering' to do extra duties. One NHS worker leaves work on time in order to collect her child from the childminder but returns to do several hours unpaid overtime during the evening.

Time off

Unlike those in other European countries, parents in Britain have no statutory right to take time off to look after sick children. Leave, both for emergencies and for routine appointments, is the most frequently mentioned provision women feel *ought* to be available at work. Women want their children's illnesses to be sufficient reason for time off in the same way as their own illnesses. The prospect of a child being ill haunts many mothers though most do not expect any concessions for this reason. Only a tiny minority is aware of any special leave entitlement at their place of work.

Flexitime is the most widely available means of juggling work hours: it is used in one fifth of women's workplaces. It enables women to make minor changes in their starting and finishing times to fit in with childcare schedules. Some women use it to build up small amounts of leave (usually not more than half a day) for taking a child to the clinic, for example. However, it rarely enables a woman to take enough time off to be with a sick child.

In practice, two thirds of women take some time off work because of their children, but of those who do, over half take only one or two days leave. Mostly this time is taken off because of children's health, and much is taken as annual leave. If a child is ill for a long period most mothers make other arrangements. Absence for only a few hours is occasionally taken unofficially, in which case women often make up the time by working lunch breaks.

Women talk about feeling compelled to pass off their absence from work for a child's illness as being for their own sickness. But six months after the return few have yet done so. One woman says 'I'd say that the car had broken down rather than the baby was ill.' Some are already saving up their annual leave in case they need to use it for this purpose. Women often express a reluctance to disclose a child's illness at work for fear of being labelled 'unreliable'.

> I said to my colleagues that I wanted a day's leave. 'I'll say the baby is ill' and they said 'Don't for God's sake say that!' I said 'Why not?' They said 'If you say that you'll get a name for yourself . . . If you're off with a cough that's OK – legitimate – but not if you're off because your son's got a temperature or chicken pox'.
>
> (*Teacher, aged 30*)

Women often say that 'No matter what, the child comes first.' In practice however, women are frequently put in the position of having to judge the severity of the child's illness and to balance this against other constraints.

> The only thing I get anxious about is when he's not well. I wish I could have time off. I hate it when he's under the weather – to have to send him to the creche. Twice I've had to send him in with his medicine. I would like to feel that when he's under the weather that I could just stop at home. (On one occasion when she did phone in to say her son was not well and asked for a

> day's leave, she met with a hostile response.) I don't think they understand at all.
>
> (*Radiographer, aged 26*)

In such cases colleagues with children sometimes cover for each other. Bosses turn a blind eye as long as women manage it successfully. One woman puts her finger on part of the solution – that *both* parents should share time off.

> I think there should be allowances but I think they should apply equally to working fathers. I think most problems occur because it's the woman who has to take time off every time the child is ill. And if men had an allowance for time off as well then it wouldn't be a problem.
>
> (*University lecturer, aged 32*)

Few women expect fathers to take time off and few do. Only one father asks for and obtains special leave. His employer, a trade union, also contributes towards the cost of a workplace nursery where the child is looked after. The parents share the time off. The wife says:

> Even at my work they gave me the nod. They said 'Take time off' ... especially as they knew that my husband was taking time off and it wasn't all falling on me.
>
> (*Secretary, aged 31*)

Bosses: helpful, unhelpful and indifferent

Given the lack of official employment practices designed to make the lot of working mothers easier, the attitudes and behaviour of bosses are critical (see Table 5.2). Only a minority facilitate women's return to work with a major concession – a transfer or a change to part-time work. Women therefore clutch at the smallest tokens of help. Here again the effects of low expectations can be seen. Although nearly half the bosses are portrayed as helpful, in reality few are reported as giving any practical support. Many women quote their bosses as suggesting that women can take time off for their children if they need to. But women do not necessarily feel that they can avail themselves of the offer, which they see as preferential treatment.

Some bosses are described as 'understanding' and 'concerned'. These tend to be men who have young children and whose wives work. They are thus able to empathize on the basis of some actual experience, albeit secondhand. Bosses can help by refraining from criticism when women first return and by not putting them under too much pressure. Women feel encouraged if they can leave work on time and are not expected to stay late. Two 'helpful' bosses gave women 'pep' talks when they went back. A confidence boost is especially important if a woman has to move to a new job on her return. None the less it is clear that many bosses, especially those in lower managerial positions, can do little in practice unless they have the support of those further up the hierarchy.

A third of bosses are described as indifferent. Some simply ignore the matter and treat women no differently from before. Others make token enquiries about women's welfare and ask polite questions about the babies.

> I would say it was tokenism. He paid lip service to understanding. That was all. He would ask about the baby but he would never ask how I coped. And he made it clear that it would not be looked on kindly if I asked to go part-time.
>
> (*Local government worker, aged 30*)

The rest – about a fifth – are seen as actively unhelpful. At the extreme end, as we mentioned earlier, a few women lost their jobs or were forced to resign after their return to work. Another suffered harassment. More commonly bosses are criticised for refusing women's requests to job share or change to part-time work. A few are hostile for no apparent reason, for example undercutting a woman's promotion opportunities purely on the grounds of her having a child. Some bosses make it clear that they do not approve of mothers of young children working. Shortly after her return to work Mary experienced a major set-back. She was contacted by the hospital nursery which her daughter attends and was asked to collect her distressed child. She took the child to the staff tearoom only to be told by her female boss to take her back to the nursery.

Work colleagues: helpful, unhelpful and indifferent

The extent to which colleagues are helpful depends at least partly upon their characters and the way the workplace is organised. In some measure support is dependent upon opportunities to reciprocate. These opportunities are more likely to occur between equals. Those who work in isolation or those who are in charge of others have no equals with whom to reciprocate. Women who are bosses themselves often feel under pressure to conceal any difficulties to do with their children. They feel obliged to 'put their job first' to set an example to those under them. However, a substantial number of women who are not in positions of authority are also reluctant to solicit help from their colleagues. 'It simply doesn't arise because I am on top of my job.' Others make a point of not bringing 'home into work'. In many cases workmates have little in common with mothers, especially those who are single, male, or older. In such cases women may make a point of not discussing their domestic situations.

A third of women say their colleagues have been helpful (see Table 5.2). Those most valued show understanding because 'they know what it's like'. Most are mothers: women with young children or those who worked when their children were young. Such women help each other out at work covering unofficially for one another if, for example, they need to slip out for half an hour to go to the creche or if they need to leave on time to collect their child from the minder at the end of the working day. Another way of being helpful is to show approval and understanding of women's situations and feelings. Women who have already returned to work after childbirth are seen as providing models to emulate.

> I was lucky that this other girl had gone back to work before me so she kind of paved the way. They'd got used to it! Before I'd left the attitude was 'Oh, we're not going to make any special allowances'.
>
> (*Social worker, aged 34*)

Over a tenth describe their colleagues as indifferent. They simply ignore the fact that women have children. Over one half of colleagues are described as unhelpful. Women who work in small close-knit groups are fortunate if there is someone in a similar situation with whom they can swap favours or feel a sense of solidarity. If there is no such person a woman often feels lonely and unsupported. Many women work in large impersonal settings with a high turnover of staff. This makes for low morale and a social climate which is distant, perfunctory and unsupportive.

Workplaces, especially offices, can be 'gossipy' places. When women decide to continue working after childbirth they are susceptible to criticism and tactless comments. They frequently forearm themselves against overt and implied criticism. Older women colleagues are often mentioned as having especially hostile attitudes towards women returners.

> A lot of older women at work think you shouldn't work with a baby especially as I waited so long to have her.
>
> (*Nurse, aged 28*)

Some suspect that this is a case of sour grapes since few older women are likely to have had the opportunity of taking maternity leave. Where women have been offered special concessions unofficially this is often interpreted by colleagues as favouritism and is likely to cause envy.

Enjoyment and importance

The story is not all bad news. Despite the absence of official employment policies most women manage to return successfully, except a very few who experience harassment at work. Almost all feel they are doing their jobs well or fairly well. Most (three quarters) find their work satisfying. Those who are unhappy tend to cite reasons to do with work. For example, teachers caught up in a protracted national dispute blame low morale and poor pay. Likewise women working in the Inland Revenue attribute diminished job satisfaction to low morale in the workplace. Asked specifically how satisfied or dissatisfied they are since having the baby, one half say it is equally satisfying as before; one quarter enjoy work more and one quarter less than before. But a significantly high proportion (two fifths) say their jobs are less important to them since the birth. Perhaps even more significantly, an even higher figure (one half) rate their jobs as being less important (to the household for example) than their husbands' jobs. Going back to work after childbirth is therefore liable to shift women's priorities but it does not appear to diminish the enjoyment they experience in their jobs.

> The job is less important than it was. (*Compared to?*) Before I had the baby. I think I could happily give it up now. To begin with I certainly did miss it and I very much wanted to go back. But now the baby is so much more fun and so much more interesting. Moneywise it's important but really that's all ... My particular job I enjoy. If I had to work in an office I think it would be a terrible drag. I wouldn't enjoy it at all. If I say I don't regard it as having the same importance that's not quite accurate. But perhaps I don't throw as much into the job as I did before ... It's a means of earning money although I do enjoy it. (*Whose job would you say is the more important in the household?*) My husband's, I suppose, because in a traditional sense he's the breadwinner. I do earn more money than he does at the moment. Nevertheless I would regard his job as the more important. (*Because?*) Because he's the man.
>
> (*Telephonist, aged 31*)

CHAPTER 6

How childcare worked out

He's settled very well. (The childminder) is lovely, she's so thoughtful. He's with a family, he's with more than just me, he gets a lot more than I could give him. And especially being my family isn't here, so he hasn't many uncles and aunts. He has quite a lively social life, which I think is very positive for him. He definitely enjoys socialising. He loves being with his minder and friend. It's astounding. I'd never have believed it.

(*Teacher, aged 29*)

On the whole, she's very nice and she does love the children. Obviously there's things the childminder does that I don't really like and I feel I can't really say too much. It's nothing really important. Well, it is important to me. She has the TV on a lot and there's sort of general things like that. I don't really feel I can say, because she's looking after him, it's her house, her TV. (*Do you ever have the chance to have a proper talk?*) No, not that much. I feel with childminders, their life carries on, they just do what they want to do. They want to be at home and it's an easy way of staying at home. I sometimes wish that Ian was the priority. I'd prefer him at a creche.

(*Telephonist, aged 30*)

SATISFACTION AND PREFERENCE

Women's feelings of guilt about leaving their child decrease once they are back at work (see Chapter 7). They are reassured by their child's reaction. Also because their experience leads them to feel that the care is adequate and, in some cases, highly satisfactory.

> I've never had any problems (with the childminder). (She and the child) get on really well. What I've got is ideal ... she's super, she's fantastic with babies.
>
> (*Primary school teacher, aged 31*)

> I'm very happy with the childminder. She's a very warm lady and also she seems to have the sort of values I have and the same kind of childrearing. I feel I've learnt from her as well.
>
> (*Social worker, aged 30*)

> I've been lucky ... (the nursery) is the only acceptable thing, I'd have given up work if I hadn't the creche. I know he's all right and that there's excellent people.
>
> (*Architect in local government, aged 28*)

> (The nanny) is brilliant with babies. He settled straightaway. I've never had any problems.
>
> (*Prison officer, aged 28*)

Women also report themselves satisfied with specific aspects of their child's care, based on a checklist of 12 items. Most say they are 'very satisfied' for each item (for full details of the checklist items and results, see Table 6.1). The four items registering most dissatisfaction are 'distance to travel to caregiver', 'cost', 'sleep, feeding and toileting' and 'the number of other children at the caregivers'.

During the first few months back at work, the proportion of women whose actual childcare arrangement is *not* what they would 'ideally' choose also decreases substantially (see Table 4.1). Now a clear majority say that their actual childcare arrangement is their 'ideal' choice. This leaves a third who would choose some change in arrangement; most of these, a quarter overall, would ideally have their child in a different type of care. Women who use childminders are still most likely to want an alternative type of care; but the proportion saying this has fallen very considerably.

THE PROS AND CONS OF 'SHARED' CARE

Virtually all mothers feel that their children gain something from the experience of 'shared' care. Three benefits are most frequently mentioned. Firstly, there are greater opportunities to mix with other children and adults, with consequent gains in sociability: some women also refer to the greater variety of activities and other experiences, as well as relationships. Secondly, it helps children to be more independent in general, and in particular less dependent on one person, the mother. Many women view such dependency as undesirable, both for themselves and for their children. Finally, mothers feel that their relationship with their child, and the quality of the time they do spend together, is enhanced. Many feel the relationship would suffer if they and their child were in each other's company all the time.

The comments that follow, from just five mothers, illustrate these positive themes, and how they often go together.

> I'm a better mother for doing it. I adore him, but I can't spend a whole day with him. By going out, I want to come home and he gets more benefit from it.

> She's seeing different people, learning to be independent, meets other children. Perhaps she appreciates me more. (The relationship) becomes something like there is between father and child.

> She's stimulated more, because of the other children and there's always something going on. He has a very full day. He knows more people and goes to playgroup. I'm not patient (so) when I see him I'm not ratty all the time. I find it easier to deal with him. I make a point of spending time with him.

> He has a better social life, goes out more. (The childminder) takes the children to school and he has contact with other children. It'll probably make him more outgoing. He gets the best of me. I make a conscious effort to play, make more of an effort (than if I was at home). I'd probably be irritable if I was home all the time.

> He gains from being with other children. I appreciate the time with him. I really enjoy our time together. He gets used to other people – not that awful one-to-one thing.

Some drawbacks are mentioned: about half the women feel that there is at least one disadvantage for their child. The most common are poorer health, the result of picking up infections from other children; a lack of individual care and stimulation, sometimes leading to slower development (thought to be most common where children are at childminders or nurseries); and, at the other extreme, being over-indulged and spoilt (invariably where grandparents have the child).

Nearly all women who cite a disadvantage also feel there are advantages in their child's care being shared. Overall, the great majority consider that 'shared' care is an unqualified benefit or that the benefits outweigh the disadvantages.

DIFFERENCES OF OPINION

Sometimes, major difficulties arise which threaten or even end childcare arrangements: these are described later in the chapter. Lesser tensions occur more commonly, even in arrangements that are viewed by mothers as basically satisfactory or even good. Rather more than half of all women report at least one instance where they have disagreed with their child's carer. Causes of disagreement vary. They include sleep, toileting, discipline and management of the child, other children at the caregivers and the hours of care: but none of these issues is mentioned by more than a few mothers.

Two issues are much more common causes of disagreement. First and foremost is food. This is mentioned by a quarter of all mothers, usually the result of mother and caregiver having different views about what the child should or should not eat. In particular, mothers feel that their attempts to establish and maintain a healthy diet are either not supported or are actually undermined.

> I probably give him more wholemeal bread, (my sister-in-law) probably gives more white bread. I'm probably more obsessed about giving him bran and vegetables ... she's essentially a working class mother, we are middle class.
>
> (*Local government solicitor, aged 29*)

Childminders and nurseries are also criticised on the same count.

> I'm not particularly happy about the food they eat (at the nursery) ... it's stodgier than I would have liked. Already she's

> developed a taste for baked beans. It's only a few weeks before she starts on hamburgers I feel.
>
> (*Secretary, aged 40*)

Biscuits, chocolates and sweets are a source of frequent disagreement. Mothers' efforts to protect their children against 'sweet, sticky' things are sometimes thwarted by caregivers.

> The only conflicting idea I have with my mother-in-law is that I think she gives too much sweet stuff ... she gives her a lot of sweet sticky things I never had as a baby.
>
> (*Senior bank clerk, aged 27*)

Other feeding issues include how – rather than what – children are fed.

> At meals, I let her hands go in the food. I feel it's good for dexterity ... (the nursery) don't allow her to do it
>
> (*Senior occupational therapist, aged 33*)

By contrast, Alice complains that her mother-in-law is not sufficiently interventionist at mealtimes.

> She spoils Louise to death. She should be drinking out of a cup, and I can't get her into proper food, because I have to take food down there. I persevere with things. (Mother-in-law) is happy to carry on.
>
> (*Bank secretary, aged 24*)

On occasion, disagreements over food are part of a more generally difficult situation. Gill left work after only two months back. By then, her relationship with her mother-in-law who cared for her son was in crisis – 'it came to a point where I'd had enough of her, I didn't want her to have the baby'. Food was one of several sources of friction.

> I went round there and said to her about giving some apple for his tea and she said 'Oh no, you don't give babies apple'. I said, 'Of course you do'. (She said) 'Well, I won't' ... and silly things like when I'd say 'Give him two Weetabix', she'd give him only one and a half ... (and) when he cried, she said 'He's got wind'

> and I said 'He's hungry' and she said 'You can't give him any more'. I said 'Yes, he'll have it, and bring it up if he doesn't want it'. It was all silly.
>
> (*Nursery nurse, aged 22*)

The second prominent cause of disagreement is the broad area of physical care and safety. The most frequent specific complaints concern nappies and keeping children warm.

> (She developed) the most appalling nappy rash. But I was able to discuss that. They weren't changing her nappy enough and they weren't using the right agents. We discussed it and it never happened again.
>
> (*Senior occupational therapist, aged 33*)

> It was fairly cold one day and she'd left him out in his pram. I don't know if I'm being protective. I just thought it was a bit cold to leave him out.
>
> (*Typing pool superintendent, aged 29*)

Where relatives are carers, and particularly where that relative is the mother's own mother, common values and background can reduce or eliminate disagreement. This is not, however, a complete guarantee. With ideas about diet and other aspects of childcare changing rapidly, a difference in generation can be a potential source of disagreement. It also seems that if children are cared for by the mother's in-laws, there is a greater likelihood of disagreements and tensions developing between mother and carer (though it is worth adding that relatives caring for children usually come from the mother's side of the family).

With childminders other factors may operate. In many cases, there is a considerable social distance between minders and mothers, which can lead to disagreements and tensions. Minders are usually also mothers themselves; but they tend to have more children and older children than the women whose children they care for, who are 'new' mothers. Childminders are also mostly working class, and have average or below average levels of education; but many of the mothers whose children they care for are in professional or managerial jobs and have high levels of education. The potential for substantial differences in values, attitude and practice is obvious.

Lack of choice in childcare also contributes to disagreement. For the few parents who use nurseries, there is little or no choice of nurseries – they use the one available to them or none at all. Similarly, while there may appear to be more choice between childminders on paper, it is unclear how far this translates into real choice. Certainly the choice is more restricted in urban areas, where more women work, and probably also for parents seeking places for a baby. In practice, few parents shop around, the great majority visiting only one childminder before making final arrangements. In these circumstances, most parents will make an overall assessment of the nursery or childminder place on offer, and decide whether it is broadly satisfactory: some difference in approach to childrearing may be the price to be paid for finding daycare for a child. A perfect or near-perfect match may occur sometimes, but in general the narrower the choice, the rougher the fit.

COMMUNICATION

Mothers may disagree with their child's carer but say nothing. The disagreements discussed so far are not always out in the open. This is part of a more general issue concerning communication between mother and carer. Just over a quarter of mothers say they would like to talk more with the child's carer, either in general or about specific subjects (see Table 6.2). The subject most commonly mentioned is how their child spends his or her day.

> (I'd like the childminder) to tell me what he's been doing sometimes. Sometimes I find out by accident. It would be nice if she actually told me ... I'd like to know – all sorts of things like what he's had for dinner, not because I want to check up ... it's just not having that control.
>
> (*Clerical officer in civil service, aged 23*)

Carers may provide vague descriptions as reassurances about a child's day, but omit the detail that the mother wants.

> I'd like to know in more detail what he's been doing ... I'd like to know what he's played with ... you tend to get 'He's been fine', but I'd like to know in more detail. They'll tell you anecdotes, but I'd like to know more about what he did.
>
> (*Teacher in a foreign language school, aged 31*)

Altogether, nearly half the mothers say they would like to talk more with their child's caregiver or that they have disagreed with her on some point, but have not said anything. Of course, there is nothing unique about the mother–carer relationship in this respect. Most of us, at some time or other, fail to raise issues or voice criticisms. This can be because we feel shy or reticent or are daunted by the person or organisation to whom we should address our views. Some mothers explained their behaviour in this way – 'I don't like confronting people, I suppose I'm a bit of a coward' or 'The nursery staff are very forceful'. On other occasions we decide not to speak out on tactical grounds: we judge that to do so will cause more trouble than it is worth. Mothers have to judge whether raising an issue will produce benefits that outweigh the possible risks or damage.

Barbara, quoted earlier as disagreeing with her 'working class' sister-in-law over diet decides not to take issue for two reasons.

> We can put emphasis on (it) at home. As long as he's happy, unless it was something big, I wouldn't make a big issue of it. She talks to her children a lot, spends a lot of time with them, she's loads more experience of being with children. (I wouldn't raise the food issue) at this stage (because) everything is running so smoothly.
>
> (*Local government solicitor, aged 29*)

In a similar situation, Jenny, who is unhappy about her childminder's use of baby talk, comes to the same conclusion and lets the matter rest.

> It's something you have to accept is going to happen. I just don't feel it's important enough (to put) a tension into the relationship that isn't there.
>
> (*Executive officer in the civil service, aged 32*)

This concern with disrupting a working arrangement is often mixed with a reluctance to hurt feelings, especially of someone who is seen as doing the mother 'a good turn'. Not hurting feelings is a particularly important consideration where the carer is a close relative.

> I thought about raising it (the amount of 'sweet stuff' parents-in-law fed to son). But I didn't want to upset her. I don't think

> she'll take any notice. She's a woman who'll carry on her own way, but she wouldn't upset me by saying 'I'm not going to do that'. If I upset her too much, and she refused to have him, it'd make life awkward.
>
> (*Senior bank clerk, aged 27*)

Alice, whose complaint that her mother-in-law does not intervene enough over her baby's feeding has already been quoted, is also reluctant to raise the issue for the same reasons. Her mother-in-law is 'doing me a good turn' – providing 42 hours of childcare for £10 a week – and Alice feels that 'I don't want to hurt her feelings'.

Particular features of the childcare situation in Britain inhibit fuller communication. The limited choice of childcare must inevitably enter the judgement of any mother deciding whether or not to raise an issue. The narrower the choice, the more reliant is the mother on the carer, and the more cautious she must be before she puts that relationship at risk.

The widespread disapproval of women with young children who go out to work must also play a part. If you feel that what you are doing is right and proper, and that you are entitled to certain standards of service, you are more likely to feel ready to raise issues and make demands. In present circumstances, many women feel 'beholden' to the caregiver for 'helping out', while uncertainty about their own lifestyle reduces their confidence in questioning the actions of others.

A final inhibiting factor particularly concerns childminding. Most childminders have young children of their own, and husbands who expect feeding and other services. Mothers whose children go to childminders are often very conscious both of these domestic demands and of the childminder's long, usually unbroken working day. Because of this, mothers can feel inhibited from taking up more of the childminder's time by raising issues or generally talking about their child.

> I'm very conscious of the fact that she has her jobs to do . . . I'm very conscious of trying to fit in with her. It's silly really – I'm paying her . . . (but) she's got responsibilities of her own, she's got three children, to give (my son) his tea earlier might not be possible. She's got to look after him. She's got the responsibility of him during the day, so it has to work to routine.
>
> (*Typing pool superintendent, aged 29*)

While such inhibitions may be felt most strongly by women who use childminders, they also operate to some extent where other types of care are used. Moreover, mothers may feel pressures themselves – from their job or home or both – which limit the time they have available to talk. Building up the relationship with the carer, and keeping the relationship going is an important task. Unfortunately, it is rarely recognised and allowed for in the organisation of working time, nor is it equally shared between parents. As we shall see, as in many other childcare areas, the responsibility and work falls largely on the mother.

CHANGING ARRANGEMENTS

Not all childcare arrangements last. In the early months back at work, nearly a fifth of mothers make at least one change. The reasons for the changes, however, vary. Different reasons have different implications and consequences.

A very few children change childcare because they and their parents move home. A second, larger group move into or out of 'temporary' arrangements. Temporary arrangements may be necessary while a more permanent arrangement is sought or until a promised permanent place becomes available. Jean, for instance, is a 32 year old nurse tutor and who returns to work when her daughter is three months old. She uses a childminder for two months until a permanent nursery place becomes available at the hospital where she works. Alternatively, temporary arrangements may be required while a 'permanent' caregiver is incapacitated for a period. Ann, a 28 year old teacher, has to move her daughter for three months to a shared nanny, while her regular childminder has a baby.

The main reason, though, for children moving is because of some problem with the childcare which requires a permanent change. There are three main problem areas. Firstly, the caregiver may stop having the child because her circumstances change. She may, for instance, get a better paid job, move house or have to stop because of ill health. In some cases, the notice given is very short.

> She did tell me at some stage that she was going to move ... but it wasn't definite. She didn't say she bought a place or anything like that. Then on the Friday when I collected him, she said 'I'll give you a week's notice because I'm leaving'. But on Monday,

> she was gone. The place was absolutely empty. It was a terrible shock. I was terribly upset.
>
> (*Playleader, aged 28*)

Secondly, some mothers move their children because they are unhappy with the care. Eva took the opportunity of a long visit from her mother to move her baby from a nursery.

> The nursery was moaning a bit about the demands she was making and I felt I've got to do something about this. And I wasn't happy about the way they were dealing with her ... (and) with the way they care for young babies. (The staff) are very young girls. They've never really had a rough time with a young baby and they don't know this is the normal pattern for a baby. They try to fit them into their routine and it doesn't work. I felt she wasn't getting the care she needed at her age. I heard stories she was left unattended and I felt guilty.
>
> (*Teacher, aged 30*)

Hannah was unhappy with her childminder, and discussed her concerns, although at this point she had not moved her son.

> I didn't think she was feeding him enough and several other things came to light which I should have picked up in the first place, but hadn't... she smoked, I honestly didn't think of it, but that played on my mind. Gradually the environment has deteriorated... and the cleanliness. She tends to send him home with porridge stains on his head. She lives in an upstairs flat and has access to a garden, but she doesn't seem inclined to take the children out very much. He's got a bit of a prison pallor.
>
> (*Physiotherapist, aged 27*)

A few weeks later, she was driven to find a new childminder.

> I didn't think she was spending as much time as she ought to. She didn't seem terribly bothered... she was also plagued with illness and I didn't think she was up to the job. I felt if it went on like that, it would start interfering with my work.

The third problem area arises when carers become disenchanted with a child. This may be because of the child's behaviour, though the mother may sometimes feel this is used as a cover for other reasons.

> Basically she said she couldn't cope. She said he was hyperactive. But it turned out she had the choice of having two children three days a week, as opposed to my son for five – which was financially a better deal and gave her two days off. She just said, 'I'm giving you one week's notice'. I felt instant panic.
>
> (*Executive officer in the civil service, aged 32*)

Alternatively carers may decide they can't cope with the way of life involved in caring for someone else's child. Julia, a 28 year old civil service clerical worker, for instance, had to move her daughter to a childminder when her mother began to find caring for a baby restricted her life too much. Another woman, Rose, describes her first nanny's sudden and traumatic disenchantment with the job, within two days of starting work.

> On the Tuesday evening, (the nanny) said she was a little bit lonely and I said I'd speak to the health visitor to see if there was any local group she could join or other nannies in the area ... (then) I got a phone call on Wednesday when I was at a meeting – 'Nanny has taken James to your mother's'. It was a *fait accompli*, and when I phoned my mother in the afternoon, she had had to come home from work because the nanny was overwrought. When I got home, my mother and the nanny were there and (the nanny) couldn't cope and was leaving and that was it. I gather I was lucky because the same college produced a girl who left two children in a house and just left ... it was a disaster, it was my most miserable time. It was so catastrophic.
>
> (*Surveyor in local government, aged 35*)

OTHER CHILDCARE DIFFICULTIES

Some childcare difficulties do not end in a move from one childcare arrangement to another. In some cases, a move is avoided by the mother leaving employment or changing from full-time to part-time work. The childcare difficulty contributes to the mother's decision, though it is usually not the only reason.

> She was becoming a bit of a handful with my mother, so there came a crisis over that. And also, when I first went back it was easy. It was much nicer than looking after her all day. But then I began to miss her and felt I wanted to spend more time with her.
>
> (*NHS planning assistant, aged 36*)

This mother can negotiate part-time work with her employer. Others give up their jobs altogether.

> Basically I gave up because I felt my baby minding arrangement wasn't satisfactory. On the one hand it was perfect because I knew she was perfectly well looked after. Who better than her two grandmas? And for the first two months things were marvellous ... he was quite happy, but the main problem was he was beginning to throw a tantrum over not getting things. So, whatever he wanted, they'd give him straightaway. They started giving him things I wouldn't want him to have. I tried to reduce his sugar intake and she'd go and buy him a sticky bun. There was interference in the way I wanted to bring him up. (He) was also suffering because they were too old for him. They were exhausted, although they didn't admit it. Things weren't active enough for him. I saw a big difference in him ... basically, I just wanted to bring him up as I want.
>
> (*Local authority housing officer, aged 28*)

Some difficulties continue unresolved for the time being, although eventually they may lead to the mother changing her employment or to the child being moved. Mostly these continuing difficulties make mothers seriously doubt the carers' ability to cope with the demands of the job or to provide adequate standards of care.

> I'd like to know more about what she does during the day. Sometimes, she will tell me, but one day I arrived very early and (my daughter) was sitting in a bouncing chair. We haven't put her in one of those for months because she's too big. The minder was cleaning out a cupboard and (my daughter) was sitting with her back to her, staring at a blank TV. That worried me a lot, but I can't bring myself to question her about it ... I also think she should have a sleep in the day, but the minder

> won't put her down for me ... I'd like another childminder, but I haven't done anything about it.
>
> (*Secondary school teacher, aged 30*)

WHICH TYPES OF CARE CAUSE MOST PROBLEMS?

Nearly a quarter of mothers have to arrange a change in childcare or experience some other childcare difficulty during their early months back at work. Childminding arrangements are most problematic. A high proportion of arrangements with relatives end in a move, but this is largely because relatives are frequently used to provide temporary care, rather than because of difficulties with the arrangement. Nurseries are most stable – very few children in nurseries are moved – and they are least likely to be reported as producing other childcare difficulties (see Table 6.3).

If, however, the indicators described earlier are considered, a different picture emerges. Nursery users appear least satisfied with their childcare, on the basis of the 12 item checklist (see Table 6.1); they more often refer to 'shared' care involving some disadvantage for their child; and they are most likely to mention a disagreement with their caregiver (see Table 6.2). There seems to be a contradiction between the stability and few major difficulties experienced by nursery users, and their relatively high level of criticism.

One possible explanation can be quickly disposed of. The great majority of women with children at nurseries are in managerial or professional jobs, a far higher proportion than among women who use relatives or childminders. But the high level of criticism voiced by nursery users is not because nurseries are used more by this group of women. If comparisons are limited only to women in professional and managerial jobs, those women using nurseries still express higher levels of criticism than those using childminders and relatives.

Three other explanations are more likely. First, there are features of the nurseries which make them liable to certain types of complaint. On the satisfaction checklist, nursery users are markedly more dissatisfied on three items – cost, distance and numbers of children – and for each of these items nursery users and their children actually fare less well. Their costs are generally higher; they have to travel further, often because nurseries are in or near workplaces; and their children are cared for in larger groups and with lower ratios of adults to children.

Second, mothers with children at nurseries may be more critical because the childcare is more public and visible. Childminders and relatives mostly care for children in their own homes. Norms of privacy and good manners concerning behaviour in other people's homes impose barriers that may make it harder to see what is going on. Women using childminders often sense that they are intruding when in the minder's house. They may feel that if they give their child to a childminder to care for, they should not interfere or pry; having made the decision, they should leave the childminder to get on with it. This, it should be emphasised, is very conjectural. We did not collect information about whether mothers using nurseries know more about the care their children receive and, if so, why.

This leads to the third possible explanation. Nurseries are not private, domestic arrangements. They are public institutions specifically for the purpose of caring for children and staffed mostly by people trained to provide such care. For these reasons, women using nurseries may have higher expectations than those using other forms of childcare.

A final point should be made. Just as the search for childcare overall seemed easier where a relative becomes the caregiver, so too childcare seemed to work out best for this group. There are of course some exceptions, but in general women using relatives appear more satisfied than those who use nurseries, and experience fewer difficulties than those who use childminders.

Some problems in assessing childcare

During the early months back at work, a substantial minority of women have to make new childcare arrangements, and a few continue to face substantial childcare difficulties. Communication between parents (or mothers) and carers is not perfect, and there are some disagreements and dissatisfactions. Despite these negative features, childcare is rarely a main or even a contributing reason for women who stop working, and most women are satisfied with the arrangements they have. Over the early months there is a process of adaptation, involving women's feelings about leaving their child in someone else's care, and sometimes also the replacement of less satisfactory childcare arrangements by rather more satisfactory ones.

How should this early experience be assessed? Before making a judgement, some additional considerations need to be borne in mind. Perhaps most important, given the predominance of private childcare, is that the most economically and socially disadvantaged parents are likely to have the least choice and the worst service (especially if they have no relatives prepared to offer childcare). This aspect, the relationship between household resources and childcare, has received little attention: the one study that attempted to take it into account concluded, in relation to childminding, 'that children of mothers born abroad and children whose mothers are in the lower occupational groups received a poorer service.' A more general point is that women make childcare decisions on the basis of the cost of care, which they consider in relation to the level of their *own* earnings rather than those of the father or household as a whole. Since women's earnings are considerably lower than men's this is a factor which is likely to keep the cost of childcare down and also adversely affect its quality.

This book does not, by and large, deal with the experiences of the most disadvantaged households – single parents, black and ethnic minority parents, parents on very low earnings. Had they been included, the picture might have looked rather different. Nor does this book attempt any independent assessment of childcare. Where this has been attempted, standards have been found to be variable, with substantial pockets of care giving real cause for concern.

There are in fact reasons why mothers' judgements of childcare may be more positive than independent ones. The inadequacies of provision in Britain, and the low level of public debate about the issues, have already been described in Chapter 1. This may lower mothers' expectations of childcare in two ways. They are less likely to be well informed about childcare services and issues; and they will be aware that alternatives are relatively few and that better places will not be readily available. Add to this women's doubts and guilt feelings about going back to work and 'leaving' their children and you have a recipe for women putting up with the limited childcare available and not taking too critical a look at the actual arrangements. As long as there is no blatant cause for concern, there is little point in scrutinising the arrangement too closely. Such scrutiny can only produce still further anxiety and guilt, with few possibilities of better arrangements.

In a more supportive situation there might have been more frequent and overt differences of opinion, more children moved by dissatisfied parents, more areas of dissatisfaction identified and expressed – though by the same token, a more supportive context may render all of this less necessary. Similarly, it becomes difficult to gauge the significance of a decreasing number of women saying they would 'ideally' choose some other type of childcare. This could reflect a genuine increase in satisfaction, a consequence of positive experience in actually using childminders or nurseries. Alternatively, it could simply be a coping strategy, of women coming to terms with, and not exploring too deeply, the one childcare solution open to them.

Finally, the type of arrangement – care by relatives – that seems on balance to create fewest difficulties with greatest satisfaction is not a universal panacea. It is neither generally available, as childminding now is, nor could it be made so, as nurseries could be. Even if it was, many parents would not wish to use it, for a variety of reasons. In the long term, it is a declining resource. Mobility of families takes a steady toll on the number of relatives available to provide care. As employment rates increase among older women, fewer women will be available or willing to look after their grandchildren.

The chapter seems therefore to suggest two conclusions. Women should not feel deterred from resuming employment by considerations of childcare: those who resume work do cope with what is available. This, however, does not justify complacency. The current situation is far from perfect. Choice is limited or non-existent, standards are variable and dependent to some degree on resources; parental expectations and critical appraisal are stifled; communications between parent and carer is often inadequate; and parents have to contend with too many needless changes and difficuties.

CHAPTER 7

What it feels like

> I'm glad I did it now. As I said before, I'd no idea what it would be like. A lot of women treat you as if you are very hard and make you feel very guilty. But I always had it in my mind that I've got to try it out. And it wasn't as bad as I'd thought. I'm pleased that I was able to survive all this. It hasn't got me down as much. I found the first three months at home so exhausting. She was very difficult and I used to feel very very alone. I was so happy the first day back – I felt I was a normal person again. It does give you something of your own ... and I was happier with my relationship with my husband. I came home, talked, happy – I wasn't snappy. So in that way it has made me more contented and I felt more interested in life ... Even if I had packed in I've still got a lot of confidence from it. You can so easily lose that. It's a horrible experience coping on your own at home. Nobody cares about you ... nobody wants to know you. But you always feel guilty, whatever you do.
>
> (*Teacher, aged 30*)

Many women see going back to work as a challenge and are prepared to experience a variety of feelings. The experience can be fulfilling and rewarding; it can also be arduous and guilt provoking – all at the same time. Women often feel very tired, especially to start with. In addition they talk about feelings of conflict, the main one being to do with the separation from their child. Yet despite these negative feelings most think they have made the right decision.

MIXED FEELINGS

Women who go back are not alone in experiencing negative feelings at this point. Women who stay at home with their children are just as likely to have some bad feelings. Furthermore, the return is not the only event which affects how women feel. Other distressing events – the illness of a friend or relation or a death in the family – can occur, not to mention more mundane problems. Bad feelings about one area of a woman's life may be offset by good feelings about another. Feelings about the same area may also fluctuate. Going back to work is a good example, some aspects of which are profoundly distressing and others highly satisfying, although some women find it difficult to recall changes in mood and, in retrospect, describe feeling 'just OK'. Shortly after her return, Janet was ill and had three weeks off. Now back at work she describes a mixture of feelings – guilt, enjoyment and guilt about enjoying herself.

> Well it's hard to say how I feel. The baby could be missing out. I feel she's not doing things she might have been doing if I'd been at home. She's not even been attempting to stand – she won't even crawl . . . I think if I'd been at home she'd have been on the floor more and encouraged . . . On the other side I feel it's done me good to go back. (*In what way?*) It's the brain power, the stimulation. Even though it's very tiring. The only time I really get doubts, except for thinking that the baby could do more, is when people look at you and say 'What are you doing back at work?' . . . It's hard to explain. I'm enjoying work and sometimes I feel guilty because I am enjoying it. And I think 'Perhaps I should be staying at home'.
>
> (*Senior bank clerk, aged 27*)

FEELINGS IN THE FIRST FEW DAYS

When women first return to work they feel acute ambivalence about leaving their children. The widespread belief that, for the first five years at least, a 'good mother' is a full-time one affects the way women *feel* even if it does not determine their decisions or views. Thus at one level a teacher thinks it 'quite all right' to go back to work but at another she feels guilty about leaving her child.

> I still have my cultural guilt about the fact that I'm not looking after him and maybe people are right when they think I should be. I enjoy my work. (*Do you think people really think that*?) Good question! An element of me thinks that and then I feel angry with myself for being so stupid as to think that. But I know when I first went back to work I felt that certain people might think I was a bad mother. And the reason I thought that as well was this voice inside me – and the guilt is still there.
>
> (*Language teacher, aged 31*)

Feelings of conflict and distress about leaving children are most likely on the first and early days of the return. Three quarters of women feel acutely distressed especially when they first leave their child with the carer.

> It seemed very odd walking around without the baby ... I used to carry her in a sling and all of a sudden I was standing on the pavement without anything. It feels as if you are missing something. I felt apprehensive, worried...
>
> (*Secretary, aged 40*)

Most women talk about feelings of loss – the feeling that they are giving up their child to someone else. Others express anxiety about their child's welfare while they are away. At the end of the working day many women can scarcely contain themselves and rush off to be reunited with their child.

Compared with the distress at leaving their children, picking up one's job again is less difficult although a number of women mention finding it hard, especially to start with.

> I certainly felt my brain had gone out the window. That's very tiring in itself. You've got to concentrate so much harder. I felt my attention span was so much less. By Monday afternoon I was knackered. Now I get to Friday lunch time ... Eight months is a long time and my job is management. You are out of touch with what has been going on.
>
> (*Senior physiotherapist, aged 34*)

COMING TO TERMS WITH THE SEPARATION

Given the intensity of their initial distress about leaving their children it is reassuring to find that a few months later most women feel markedly different (see Table 7.1). Once the children are 10 to 11 months old the great majority have come to terms with the situation and have largely overcome their sadness and worry.

> I really felt in that first week as if my heart was breaking – leaving her. I thought 'I'm never going to get over this'. But it's got much easier now. It's a bit like a broken love affair, I suppose. It mends.
>
> (*Teacher, aged 29*)

Coming to terms with the separation from the child is described in similar terms to the process of grief following a death. Initially women are overcome with the trauma of separation and anguish at the physical absence of the child. With time and the realisation that the child is happy and settled at the carer's and shows no obvious signs of missing them, they accept the separation, although guilt feelings recur from time to time.

> Leaving him was a wrench. I'm not sure if it was depression or what. Or whether it was a sort of selfish feeling. I just missed him. It was worst at the time I had to drop him off. I was running to the tube crying my eyes out. It was a difficult time those first two weeks. I had been very obsessed with the baby. Obviously he's the main thing in my life. But he's not the only thing I ever think about now. I'm forced to think of other things. (*Do you feel OK about that*?) I think so. He still has all my love and loads of attention. Now I don't worry at all about him at work. At first it was difficult because I had to come to terms with my relationship to the baby. (*Did you feel guilty*?) Yes, I think you do. I think most of us would.
>
> (*Assistant solicitor, aged 29*)

Another mother eventually overcomes the not uncommon fear that the baby may forget who her or his mother is.

> It was a lot easier than I thought it would be. I had fantasies in my head that nobody else could look after the baby. Nobody

> will do it in the same way which is a load of nonsense. The baby survives willy nilly.
>
> (*Doctor, aged 34*)

The next mother accepts the situation but sometimes feels guilty that she is enjoying being back at work.

> I'm enjoying work but I sometimes feel guilty because I am enjoying it and I think perhaps I should be staying at home. The first day back was dreadful. I'll never forget it. I came home and all I could do was cry. I felt awful. I found it very hard – the first couple of weeks. (*Did it go on*?) No, it didn't actually. The first day was really the shocker. It brought home to me that I wasn't going to be with the baby any more. Then after that it became easier because I became involved in work. And at work I managed to cut myself off from home and the baby ... but the first day I was so scared she might have forgotten who I was – that she might not remember I was her mother. But I got over that when I realised she wouldn't forget. (*How do you feel now*?) It's all right. (*Any pangs*?) None at all. (*What about guilt*?) Only that first day. Now it's easier.
>
> (*Senior bank clerk, aged 27*)

It is almost always mothers who do the dropping off and collecting of the child. This does not help their adjustment: in these two latter cases, the fathers take the children to and from the carers and the mothers feel less guilty about 'leaving' them.

RECURRING GUILT FEELINGS

If acute feelings of conflict persist women usually give up work altogether or change to part-time hours. Only a handful do so and, almost always, other factors are also part of the decision.

Feelings of conflict can recur from time to time, especially when children are ill or off colour. It is usually the mother who is faced with the dilemma of how to cope: five months after returning to work two thirds of mothers have taken some time off because of their children, as compared with only a third of fathers. If the illness is only slight, women are reluctant to use up precious annual leave which they want to reserve for the occasions when the carer is unable to have the child or the child is 'really' ill. If the mother decides the child is fit enough to go to the minder's she often feels bad about it.

> I suppose there's still the odd doubt, especially if he's got a cold and he's not well. I think times like that when he's not very well, I think 'I wish I didn't have to go to work'. I'd rather be at home ... Just when he's not well and it's very cold ... You do feel a bit guilty.
>
> (*Radiographer, aged 26*)

Guilt is sometimes experienced fleetingly, induced by a reminder of how a 'proper mother' ought to behave.

> On sunny days when I see lots of mothers and their babies – there's a playschool nearby – I think 'I really should be with him'. I feel guilty.
>
> (*Bank clerk, aged 26*)

Women can be vulnerable to such feelings when they have time to think. As this mother whose child is cared for in a workplace nursery said:

> When I'm busy I'm happy and when I'm not I sit there thinking 'I could be downstairs with the baby'.
>
> (*Local government administrator, aged 31*)

A major source of guilt or other negative feelings is the worry that someone looking after the child might not invest as much effort as the mother feels she would.

> I thought to myself 'Is he going to fall down the stairs? Is he going to do this?' I had visions of her leaving him on the settee. I was wondering 'What if she leaves the door open and he tries to climb the stairs and gets half way up and falls?'
>
> (*Security clerk, aged 22*)

The strong sense of responsibility mothers feel for their children's welfare makes them want to compensate for their absence when they get home from work. If, because of tiredness or having other things to do, they aren't able to devote their time to them they feel guilty.

> Just in the last week I've begun to feel guilty about not being with the baby. At weekends I don't feel I'm fulfilling the baby as much. Because I'm tired and I'm not really giving the attention I should.
>
> (*Hospital cook, aged 20*)

OTHER FEELINGS

Women experience other negative feelings as well as guilt (see Table 7.2). A few are jealous of the child's carer. Others feel rejected – 'a bit left out' – if, for example, the child doesn't rush into their arms when they come to collect him or her. However, this feeling is often balanced out by relief as the woman realises that the child is happy and has a good relationship with the carer.

> I feel a bit worried sometimes when I go into my Mum's and 'Mummy's here' and she takes no notice. (*Do you feel rejected?*) Yes, and sometimes she goes to my Mum quite a lot and I feel she's pushing me out. My sister explained that she used to feel jealous also when my Mum used to look after my little nephews and nieces...
>
> (*Bank clerk, aged 26*)

Some mothers are worried at first about losing control over the child – that they might cease to be the major influence in their child's life.

> I still doubt if I should be (at work) because of the child. I'm not sure I like her at the nursery ... I just wanted to be aware of what she was getting, what stimulation. I suppose I wanted control over her babyhood. I felt I was handing her over ... I was worried she wouldn't get the sort of care I might have given her ... It's an emotional thing – it's your baby and you want to look after it and protect it.
>
> (*Teacher, aged 29*)

Even if a woman doesn't doubt the carer's ability to look after children or her concern, at times she may feel a strong desire to look after her child herself.

> There's a sense of disappointment in not being able to stay with her. I went back to work not just because I wanted to but because my husband was made redundant ... It's not guilt because she's not suffering.
>
> (*Secretary, aged 24*)

On the whole women feel the losses to be mainly their own rather than their children's though they may not feel this all the time.

> Mondays are always the worst. When I get to Friday I'm used to it ... I feel a bit upset because I've so enjoyed him over the weekend and got used to him and got close to him. I miss him more and I don't want to leave him.
>
> (*Clerk, aged 23*)

TIREDNESS

As well as being predominant in the period following the birth, tiredness is a major feature of the early months back at work. One third are more tired than before whereas only a fifth are less tired (see Table 7.3). About half report the same degree of tiredness. Just over one half of women who do not resume work also report the same degree of tiredness at this stage as earlier, but otherwise the picture is roughly the reverse, with more women becoming less tired. For those going back to work the type of occupation appears to have little effect on how tired they are.

Melinda grew more tired after the return to work. Whilst on maternity leave she said:

> Some days I feel great and some days I do get tired. Some days I feel really good and I decide to go out and enjoy myself. And then I pay for it. If I get to bed early and look after myself I'm usually all right ... It's a bit of a drain but I'm not usually exhausted or anything like that.

After her return she attributes the increase in tiredness to stress and lack of support at work.

> Yes. I get extremely tired. I wasn't that tired before I went back ... not every day. I suppose there are some days when I feel fine

> but most days at the moment I feel quite shattered because it's getting me down and it's got worse. When I first went back I thought 'I'm doing really well and I'm coping very well'.
>
> (*Play leader, aged 28*)

Some women feel only mildly tired before and after the return. A local government administrator is relatively untroubled on maternity leave especially since her baby settled well at night from the very beginning. After her return she says:

> I'm tired but just at the end of the week. On Thursday or Friday I feel tired. But by the time I've driven home and totally changed what I'm doing I find that gives me a totally new lease ... And in some ways I feel less tired now. Your mind is quite active. I find I'm doing more and I almost find I can cope better with the household chores than when I was at home.
>
> (*Local government administrator, aged 29*)

For some, tiredness is reduced once they are back at work. Another local government administrator was very tired on maternity leave, mainly because the baby had colic and never slept through the night. She described him as a very difficult baby. While on maternity leave she said:

> My problem is a sort of fatigue. I'm getting better but I suppose it is sort of every day. By five o'clock I'm quite tired and a little bit cross. If my husband gets home at a normal time and if he can take the baby for an hour I can recover. But otherwise I'm just whacked. I just can't be bothered to do anything. I just flop. It's a loss of strength. Some of it must be mental stress in trying to keep the baby occupied all day.

Six months later she says:

> I'm getting better but certainly up to Christmas I was getting very tired in the evening ... When you're back at work you think you're tired but inevitably ... By the time you've gone through the routine of what you've got to do with the baby I just sit down with a cup of coffee after the meal and that's it – I'm straight out! I think I'm probably less tired. When you came last time I was still in the bad period. It did get better.
>
> (*Local government administrator, aged 35*)

Types of tiredness

Women are clearly subject to different stresses in different situations and their tiredness varies in quality as well as quantity. Feeling tired when your baby is five months old may be a hangover from the birth. Young babies can also be emotionally and physically demanding and many wake regularly in the night to be fed. At 10 to 11 months they may still be waking at night, an added strain for women who have had a long day at work. In well over half the cases mothers do the getting up. Just under a third share it with their husbands, leaving only nine per cent of fathers who do it alone.

The initial period back at work is likely to be a stressful time since women are unused to doing their jobs and, in addition, may have to cope with changes at work which have occurred in their absence. Coming back to work after a couple of weeks' holiday can be difficult but a break of several months is much more so. It is perhaps surprising that not more women feel tired.

Being at home and being at work produce different kinds of tiredness. Being at home can often induce lethargy or boredom because of being tied to the house all day. In this situation tiredness is the result of repetitive mundane domestic chores and of routines unbroken by much social contact. Women frequently contrast this type of tiredness with tiredness from being at work – the feeling of overload from trying to combine responsibilities on both domestic and work fronts.

> By the end of the day I'm ready for my bed ... I think it's physical – doing a full-time job, running a home and looking after a baby ... I think when I was at home it was more that I was tired out of boredom. Now it's more the exhaustion. I'm more tired now but it's a different sort. Before it was mental, now it's physical.
>
> (*Supervisor in a typing pool, aged 22*)

Going back to work is often described as physically exhausting especially in the first weeks. This may be exacerbated by a long and difficult journey to work involving detours to the child's carer. For example, a teacher has to drive 15 miles from an outlying suburb to her school in central London. On the way she drops the child off at a private nursery near home and collects her after work.

> The feeling of being absolutely exhausted ... The first two or three weeks I just couldn't stop. I'd come home and rush about and keep the house beautiful and cook meals. I was really high. When I came down it was a bit of a shock ... I found I was living for the weekend. It was more *physical* tiredness. The first week I nearly killed myself driving in and out of central London. As soon as the bell went I was out and I was driving so fast. I thought 'This is ridiculous. Life will wait five minutes for you'.
>
> (*Teacher, aged 29*)

Some women *prefer* feeling physically tired from working hard to feeling lethargic at home.

> I used to feel tired because I was indoors. *Now* it's a nice sort of tiredness. You can go to bed and sleep. It's through actually *doing* something rather than being stuck in the house. I'm usually tired in the evening by the time I get home and sort everything out. I don't usually sit down very early, but by the time I do I feel quite worn out.
>
> (*Clerk, aged 22*)

A supermarket cashier who recently gave up her job because her mother, who used to look after the baby, is moving finds being at home depressing as well as tiring.

> I do get very tired. If I sit there once the baby is off I think to myself 'I could go to sleep.' Now I'm at home ... it's making me feel as if I'm just a housewife. Just there to cook and clean and look after the baby. Some days I think 'Oh! Just the same again.' It gets me down. I think it's because I've been used to working all this time. Sometimes I do wake up feeling a bit depressed.
>
> (*Cashier, aged 20*)

Combining work and parenthood is not only physically tiring, it also involves a lot of mental stress, especially since the responsibility and organisation fall mainly on women (see Chapter 9). Over a third of women say that they would like more responsibility taken off their shoulders. Nearly two thirds of the women spend over nine hours each day out of the house, and childcare and domestic work involve considerable time and energy at the end of an already long working day. It is not really surprising that they feel tired.

POSITIVE FEELINGS AND EVALUATIONS

Women also mention feeling positive about going back to work. Asked to make an overall judgement about their decision to return, four fifths of the women are on balance positive. The rest are negative or mainly negative (see Table 7.4). In considering the benefits three major themes emerge.

Firstly, they consider their children's happiness. Despite their ambivalence about 'leaving' their children, most mothers (four fifths) feel that on balance their children gain from daycare.

Secondly, women feel they have made the right decision because it makes them 'better mothers'. Their children benefit because they are more patient with them. Going back to work makes them appreciate their children more and they feel that their relationships with them have been enhanced.

> I think because I have time away from him the time I have with him is more valuable and I try to be more patient. If I were with him all day and every day I'd be more fraught and he'd be shut up in his cot more often. And it gives him the chance to meet this other little girl at the minder's whom he gets on with really well and to meet other people which I think is really important.
> (*Surveyor, aged 28*)

Thirdly, women feel that they are doing the 'right thing' because they themselves are happier. Some women talk about feeling less bored when they are in the company of their children. Others feel that having an interest beyond motherhood and not being with their children all the time enables them to be more stimulating and attentive when they are with them and so to enjoy them more. Moreover both parties are said to benefit – mother and child. As one woman says, their time together is 'qualitatively better' since she has been back at work. Another says:

> It does make me look forward to seeing her in the evening and to giving her lots of attention. I enjoy it. I really do want to see her. That time we have is probably deeper than some mothers

> have who are at home all day with their children ... And because I'm happier everyone is happier.
>
> (*Teacher, aged 30*)

How this improvement in the relationship works is not precisely clear. In some cases it is the fact that women come home fresh to their children in the evening while, in others, the company at work and the interest of the job clearly stimulate them and make them 'better' mothers and 'happier' people. As one woman comments, 'I'm better through seeing people. So I think I'm a lot nicer to the baby.' Another feels that working makes her feel good in herself which in turn reflects on her role as a mother.

> I find it very very relaxing – like a breath of fresh air – time to myself and the fact that I haven't got him wingeing round my legs. When I see him I appreciate him an awful lot more. I have more patience with him.
>
> (*Audiology technician, aged 24*)

As we noted earlier, being at home on maternity leave is not a particularly happy experience for many women. Fearing that a miserable mother who stays at home may be worse for a child than a happy mother who goes to work, some think they will never discover the truth unless they try it out. For most the experience has proved positive despite the conflicts and the tiredness.

> I feel I really know what I want now, and I have more of an idea of what is good for the baby.
>
> (*Industrial journalist, aged 30*)

An improvement in one's performance at work is a further benefit. They put it down to a renewal of self confidence and the sense of challenge and achievement in having 'managed' the return. Three quarters enjoy working as much or more than before the birth.

> I could use words like happy, confident. And I do feel fulfilled. I've got lots of interesting things to do. I enjoy what I'm doing ... I was quite excited really about the challenge. It was really quite invigorating to be back and feel I could work again. I felt my old self ... For my self esteem it's worked out for the better – to feel I could go back into the same situation and function

> more or less at the same level even when I'm dog tired. It's something that's been quite good to do.
>
> (*Clinical psychologist, who returned part-time, aged 30*)

Feelings do not lend themselves to a neat 'cost-benefit' exercise: it is not easy to indicate the relative balance of positive as against negative feelings. However, on the whole women evaluate their return in positive terms and cite a number of benefits to their children and themselves.

CHAPTER 8

How women cope

> I'm coping very well indeed . . . I've probably coped better than I thought I would . . . I'm very proud of the fact I'm a working mother and it's working because you go into it with such fears. You think 'Will I be able to cope?'
>
> (*PE teacher, aged 29*)

Women cope with their return to work in different ways. On the whole most (nearly two thirds) feel they are coping as well as they would like (see Table 8.1). This is not to say that they necessarily admit to 'having problems' when they resume work, although clearly there are some aspects of going back which are difficult, at least to start with. As the last chapter describes, women find it hard to leave their children. In addition, just over half the women mention one other issue they find difficult to cope with. Most frequently mentioned are managing the housework and the general work overload of combining employment and motherhood. Two other frequently mentioned problems are unhelpful circumstances at work and difficulties with childcare, which are dealt with in Chapters 5 and 6 respectively.

WHAT DOES COPING MEAN?

Coping has been described as 'the things that people do to avoid being harmed by life's strains'. This definition may have a narrow meaning, referring only to the ways people psychologically 'protect' themselves from unpleasant experiences. It can also be extended to cover the problems with which they have to contend, together with their practical and emotional responses to them.

People cope with crises and trauma but they also have to cope with more mundane and routine experiences. Coping is also something that women and specifically mothers do and are expected to do. Working mothers cope largely unaided. They take it for granted that the main responsibility for managing jobs, children and homes is theirs. Few cope by sharing the workload with their partners or other people. If husbands contribute to housework or childcare they are described as 'helping'. Even in cases where husbands give quite a lot of help women say it would be nice to have a cleaning lady or their mother or a neighbourhood 'auntie' to come in and tidy up. Only a few have paid domestic help. Whether or not they get much help women tend to feel that they ought to do the housework themselves. They can only do so by lowering their standards and this they find difficult to do at first. Eventually they come to accept a drop in standards but not without regretting that the house is not as clean and tidy as they would like it to be.

People outside the immediate family are called on to assist only in emergencies. A third of women say they find it difficult to ask for or to accept help from other people. In the event only a handful get help from anyone other than their husbands on a regular basis. Self-reliance pervades the language in which women voice their experiences. Combining full-time employment with motherhood means juggling diverse responsibilities which they see as essentially their own.

> I find I'm a split personality. When I go to work I have to be one person – pretend I'm efficient and on top of everything. When I come home it's like I'm a different person ... I'm still like the same person I was before I had the baby but I have all these extra responsibilities ... I don't feel I'm coping as well as I should. I feel I'm old before my time.
>
> (*Clerical worker in the civil service, aged 23*)

Women play down any resentment they feel, accepting that it is largely 'up to them' to find the time and energy to cope. And most do. Nearly one half of women say that they feel they have coped quite well and a further two fifths well or very well (see Table 8.2).

With the taking on of responsibility go *feelings* of responsibility and of guilt if the work is not done. Because mothers in Britain are supposed to stay at home, women who opt for a different pattern of mothering are particularly likely to feel guilty and also to be criticised by others.

Women who resume work after childbirth cope in three ways. Firstly, they organise and carry out the *practical* everyday tasks involved in the complex web of caring for children, doing their jobs and looking after the home. Secondly, they develop ways of *viewing* their new lives as working mothers which enable them to accommodate to the necessary changes in lifestyle. Thirdly, they cope with any negative *feelings* – namely guilt and the feeling of missing out on their children.

PRACTICAL STRATEGIES

At a practical level women can only manage to be both mothers and full-time workers by economising on time and energy, and they are only too well aware of the scarcity of these resources. The purpose of saving these resources is to devote them to their children. They cut down on social life and housework in order to spend more time with their babies. Indeed most activities in women's lives outside employment, motherhood and the home go by the board.

Housework strategies

Most women are concerned with being organised when they go back to work. They try to plan ahead and use their time economically. Many women start by trying to fit in as much housework as before, but as time goes on, a high proportion cut down on chores or lower their standards. Not many stick to their old routines, although a few work even harder in the house (see Table 8.3).

Those who attempt to 'do everything' at first soon get very tired, although there are some exceptions. Samantha continues to keep up standards by sticking to her former routine. She is helped by being within walking distance of both her work and the minder and she has a very organised approach to life.

> It's only about six weeks now that I've been back at work and I do feel at times 'Can I cope? Or is it going to be too much?' ...

> All the time I'm thinking 'Have I got things ready for the next day, are we straight here?' And keeping up with the washing and ironing and this sort of thing. . . . It's just that I want to get it straight in my own mind. I'm very much for routines anyway – doing things by certain times – . . . I'm a stickler for time-keeping. I've never been the sort of person to stay in bed and let the day drift by.
>
> (*Clerical worker, aged 35, who returned early*)

Some months later, she says:

> It's all working out nicely, the house doesn't suffer. I feel I'm back on to doing the same things around the house as before we had the baby.

However, after a while many women make a conscious effort to lower their standards and cut corners. Some women make special efforts to get the housework done during the week, thereby leaving the weekend free to spend with their child. Others say they spend one day at the weekend catching up.

> I want to spend the time with the baby. I don't want to do housework . . . I try to get everything done on a Saturday, so I've got Sunday free . . . It's down to me to actually get on and do it.
>
> (*Clerical assistant, aged 32*)

One of the more common corners women cut is the ironing. Some stop cooking a main meal at night and have a hot dinner at the works canteen and try to ensure that their partners do the same. Only a few women mention purchasing convenience foods such as ready-made meals.

Another strategy for coping with housework is to become 'more organised'.

> I just find I'm much more organised than I used to be. I've got more of a daily routine than I ever used to have and a sort of weekend routine – certain things have to be done . . . Even though it goes against my nature . . . (*What sort of things?*) The day to day things like getting up and getting organised in the

morning and weekend – getting all the shopping done and also getting things done while he's asleep.

(*Infant school teacher, aged 37*)

Giving *thought* to organisation is one way of coping. For example, women who have to be organised at work try to bring some of these skills to bear at home. At the same time women set a high premium on flexibility in order to avoid disappointment if they fail to achieve their goals. A local government officer takes her child to the workplace creche on the train into central London during the rush hour. Before resuming work she does a number of 'dummy runs'.

My sort of job you've got to be fairly well organised. Well you don't have to be but it's easier if you are. You can bring some of those skills into being a working Mum. I am always working out what to do next – how much time I've got and how much I'm going to get done. Silly things like what she's going to wear in the morning, and checking what I want to wear is clean. Leaving enough time to do everything and leaving enough time to switch off ... If things do go wrong you've got to grin and bear it. The only time I do fall down is if I plan to do something and it doesn't work out and then I feel annoyed with myself for expecting it to.

(*Local government officer, aged 31*)

In the last 30 years there has been a technological revolution in the home which is supposed to have alleviated much of the burden of housework – automatic washing machines, freezers, dishwashers and the like. Labour saving appliances are as common in single earner households as dual earner ones. Almost everyone has an automatic washing machine and a freezer; only half have tumble dryers and one tenth dishwashers. However, very few women mention them as helping them to cope.

Dual and single earner households do however differ in their access to cars. Nearly three quarters of women in professional and managerial occupations and just under half of women in other jobs either have their own cars or access to the 'family car' most of the time. Less than one half of women at home have such access. For those women who resume work, cars are of great importance since it is they who have the responsibility for taking the children to and from the carers. Cars are convenient: for conveying the women to and from work quickly and for transporting the children comfortably, especially in bad weather. They are also useful for taking all the children's equipment, food and toys to and from the carers' homes.

Social life

Almost four fifths of women say they have cut down on social life (going out, visiting friends, entertaining at home), hobbies and other interests. Women who are out at work see rather fewer people on a regular basis than mothers who are still at home. Given that keeping up with friends and kin is more often than not women's responsibility they have little time or energy for such pursuits.

Working mothers not only give up entertaining at home, they also refrain from socialising with colleagues at work. They often work through their lunch hours and they rarely go out with workmates after work.

> I opted out of all the office Christmas parties bar two. Whereas people would plead with me, 'Oh come on!', if the chips were down, I'd rather go home and have that hour with the baby.
>
> (*Local government officer, aged 35*)

> We've given up things that weren't terribly important. We don't mind not going out and we don't mind going to bed early.
>
> (*Librarian, aged 34*)

Women don't necessarily resent the lack of a social life at this time. Since the birth they have already become accustomed to restrictions upon their activities. Moreover they believe that this is one of the costs attached to combining work and motherhood.

Reorganising time

Women are much less happy about a different kind of loss – namely the lack of time to themselves. This is seen as a minimal requirement given that they forego most areas of 'choice' in their lives. Just over four fifths feel they do not have enough and almost a third are unhappy about it.

'Going to bed early' is the most frequently mentioned strategy for saving energy. Unlike getting up early, which is taken for granted, going to bed early represents a conscious choice.

> Like going to bed early you mean? That's at the heart of it I think ... It's just a kind of shifting your clock. Before I would go to bed say at 12.00 and get up at 7.00. Now I'll go to bed at 10.00 and get up at 6.00.
>
> (*Librarian, aged 34*)

A clerical worker saves time in the morning by spending less effort on her appearance. This she is happy to do since, in becoming a mother, she has a new image of herself which precludes the glamour of make-up. Spending more time with her child helps to alleviate feelings of guilt about 'leaving' her.

> I always used to make sure when I went out of the house that I was made-up and nicely dressed. Now I just don't worry about the make-up. (*Why?*) When she was young I didn't like to just sort of leave her down there on the floor while I was up there making-up ... And I put the make-up aside and thought 'Right. She's more important' ... Going back to before I had the baby – if I'd have gone to work without make-up then I'd have worried about what people would say. Now it doesn't matter to me any more.
>
> (*Clerical worker, aged 35*)

MENTAL ATTITUDES

With the change in their lives that going back to work involves, working mothers often adopt new attitudes that ease the transition. These include an easy-going acceptance of life; trying to make up for difficulties by compensating children, employers, husbands and themselves; compartmentalising the two worlds of work and home; and thinking positively about their decision to work. These may sometimes seem contradictory, but in fact represent a rational response to the contradictory demands that working mothers face.

Taking life as it comes

Becoming more organised and cutting corners with the housework are strategies that some women have to work at. Similarly adopting a more relaxed approach to life goes against the very grain of some people's personalities, habits, and deep-seated feelings. Even so four fifths of women attempt 'to take life as it comes' both in relation to the housework and also in their lives generally. A theatre sister describes reversing her former way of coping.

> I don't know whether I said this when I last saw you. But before we had the baby things *had* to be done. If I say it has to be done today it's got to be done today. But now I'll leave it till the next day and it won't bother me. And that really does make a difference. I mean my *whole* attitude is now that way. Obviously it's not that way at work ... But when I get home I enjoy this freedom I've given myself. It's quite nice ... I was terribly precise at one time ... But I changed. It happened very gradually. But I did notice I'm different. Why worry? I'll do it tomorrow. It's going to get done.
>
> (*Theatre sister, aged 29*)

A radiographer is managing to change her ways to some extent. Putting away the baby's toys after he is in bed is a sign that the baby hasn't entirely taken over her life:

> Well, my attitudes have changed completely. Nothing's worth getting het up about any more. I used to get very het up about the slightest little thing whereas now I don't for some reason ... Nothing seems to worry me quite so much as it used to. (*When did it change?*) When he was six months old. That was the next milestone for me ... he could sit up and you could give him a toy to play with. It was very important to me to keep the house clean and tidy and it was very difficult because he was the sort of baby that wanted attention all the time ... It was very important, and still is, once he's gone to bed I make sure this room is toy free and things are put away. I just didn't want the house to be completely baby-oriented. It's still a home. It's still somewhere where we can relax. It was very important to me that the house wasn't going to become messy and dirty because we've got a baby.
>
> (*Radiographer, aged 26*)

Compensating for being a working mother

Women's main concern on their return to work is that their children will not suffer, either from a lack of attention from the carers or from themselves. Not surprisingly, women try to compensate their children for their absence by devoting as much time to them as possible when they are together and by ensuring that this time is of a high quality.

> When I go home – she doesn't go to bed 'til 7.45 – I devote that time to her. I just leave everything because I haven't been with her all day and I think 'This is her time' and she would get irritable if I wasn't playing with her . . . During that time she has her supper and we play and I really enjoy that time.
>
> (*Nursing officer, aged 31*)

When Stella is with her baby, she is very conscious that he may pick up the 'vibes' of being in a rush.

> I think he knows it as well if I'm always on the run. So I have tried to take it a bit more easy. I think things have really just happened . . . I've tried to make sure I bath the baby once every other night and I make a point of doing that. It's a nice time and he enjoys his bath . . . And I've tried to set the time aside to play with him because otherwise he just wouldn't get any attention. So I have to be careful about that . . . I see how I go – what time I get in. If he's tired I wouldn't bother – just give him a quick cuddle. But I usually give him tea, play with him and give him a bath.
>
> (*Clerical assistant, aged 23*)

The success of this strategy is shown by the fact that four fifths of the women feel that working has enriched their relationship with their child to some or to a great extent. But even so nearly two thirds feel that they ought to be spending more time with their child.

Women are also conscious that they are compensating themselves as much as their children. Some devote so much attention to them that they feel they are excluding their husbands.

> I suppose I'm very selfish with my time – I don't see the baby all the time. When I do I spend all my time with him which actually

> isn't very good because my husband does mind ... I don't suppose I should put the baby first.
>
> (*Nurse, aged 29*)

Working mothers seek to compensate in other ways. Fearing the label of unreliability so often attached to working mothers they try to compensate their employers by being even more conscientious in their work. They sacrifice their own interests by taking virtually no time off for their own illness and by saving up their holiday in case their children are ill. They are concerned to appear to be coping well, especially in the first weeks. One way of achieving this is not to confess to difficulties.

> I didn't let on to anybody around how I was feeling. I'd never have dreamed of confessing that because I did not want people to think 'Here comes a mother back to work. Get back to your house, dear.' OR 'Of course we shouldn't take on people after babies.' I didn't want anyone to have the opportunity to say 'Ah! It never works!'
>
> (*Local government administrator, aged 35*)

In addition to compensating their children and their employers women sometimes seek to compensate themselves. They usually do so in the context of being a couple. They want to ensure that their relationships with their partners will not suffer because they work. One of the consequences of having a young child and of working full-time is that women have less time alone with their partners and little opportunity for going out together despite the presence of two incomes. When they go out they go 'as a family' rather than as a couple. Indeed some mothers say they would feel 'even more guilty' leaving their children with babysitters. Women often organise 'treats' at home. Typically it is the mothers' earnings that are spent on treats since it is their absence rather than their husbands' for which compensation must be made.

> We have lots of treats because I think 'I am working' and we can afford it. So we ought to be spending this money now at a difficult time. Because it *is* a difficult time while she is very small. And we don't think twice about buying something if we want it ... if we wanted a special toy for the baby we'd just get it. That's important to treat yourself – with food and things like

> that. (*Now rather than in the future?*) Yes – much more for the moment. We used to go out quite a lot to restaurants ... We can't now. I would tend to buy smoked salmon and prawns now and things for Saturday evenings for our supper – so we don't sort of think 'We're sitting here eating fish and chips'.
>
> (*Nursing Officer, aged 31*)

Compartmentalising two worlds

A further strategy for coping with the twin demands of motherhood and employment is to keep them separate. Women are conscious that the worlds of employment and motherhood are only divided in time and space. At work women still think of themselves as mothers and as having responsibility for their children. At home they are conscious of the importance of their employment to household income. Because of the interdependence of the twin spheres of work and home women feel a compelling need to separate them in their *heads*. It is in this rather than in the more literal sense that women talk about 'not taking the baby into work'.

Almost all the women agree with the general statement that working mothers should try to leave their work problems at work and their domestic problems at home. In practice once back at work the great majority say they have little difficulty in keeping their minds on the job. A similar proportion say they leave their work behind them when they go home at night.

> I do compartmentalise a bit more. I have work time and I have home time and that manifests itself by not bringing my work home so much ... Now it really has to work very clearly – work and home. Now I work only when he's being minded ... If I work from home I tot up the hours that I do ... I think I value the time I'm putting in more. Whereas before I let work spill over into every corner of my life and I really didn't achieve more. It forces me to do things efficiently.
>
> (*Clinical psychologist, aged 30*)

On the whole where people are able to keep separate their various activities they are greatly assisted by a transitional period in the structure of their day. For many working mothers the opportunity to 'switch off' from work is limited to the time they spend travelling between the workplace and the child's carer. When women arrive home they have little chance to disengage from their work roles as they have to take over the home role immediately.

A positive attitude – wanting it to work

Given that so many features of working motherhood are not within the power of women alone to change – the world of employment, the division of childcare and housework – it is not surprising that women emphasise the importance of adopting positive attitudes (see Table 8.4).

> And wanting it to work. Having a very positive attitude and expecting it to work. I think that does an awful lot and if you don't it will be difficult because you'll be almost looking for problems.
>
> (*Local government administrator, aged 29*)

Women think positively by emphasising the advantages of their working for themselves and their children. For themselves it is beneficial to their role as mothers, for example by making them more patient. In Chapter 6 women describe daycare as being beneficial: dwelling on the possible benefits for their children as well as themselves is one of the ways of coming to terms with 'leaving' them.

> I've tried to look at all the positive things. I think he's more contented, more stimulated. I suppose I've justified it to myself – that he is gaining from it, as well as me ... Emotionally you feel it's wrong. But you know you have got to work for the positive and try to make it work ... It's a way of coping with the guilt.
>
> (*Librarian, aged 24*)

COPING WITH FEELINGS

In addition to coping with the demands of working motherhood women have to cope with their feelings of stress and distress. In Chapter 7 it emerged that the chief negative feeling women experience on resuming work is aroused by their separation from the child. Most women come to terms with the separation fairly quickly although feelings of guilt, conflict, loss and general ambivalence do return from time to time and in particular kinds of circumstance. Women cope with this distress in different ways at different times.

Avoidance

One way is to avoid dwelling on negative feelings and their source. Hence women may put a lot of effort into learning not to think too much about their children while they are away. The strategy of avoiding distressing thoughts is in turn assisted by the strategy of keeping the two worlds of work and home separate.

> When I first went back I'd think about what she was doing and be upset. But I soon learnt that the only way to do it was not to think about her. (*Were you able to*?) Oh yes. Occasionally I'd think about her but I can cope with it now because I know she's settled.
>
> (*Teacher, aged 29*)

By contrast, women do not have to make a great deal of effort to concentrate on their jobs when they resume work. Any difficulty they experience tends to occur in the first weeks and they soon learn how to avoid unneccessary worry.

Women are often surprised at how quickly old routines at work reassert themselves and how readily they learn to 'switch off', though in some cases switching off is itself a source of guilt feelings.

> I can cope quite well at school forgetting her but I feel guilty forgetting her at the end of the day.
>
> (*Teacher, aged 30*)

Acceptance

Women alleviate their distress by accepting the fact that they are missing out on some aspects of their babies' development or by simply accepting that it isn't possible to be with them all the time.

Acceptance is not usually achieved immediately: it has to be worked at. Even so ambivalent feelings may persist.

> As far as looking after the baby is concerned, well we went through a phase – But again, now, we *accept* it. We came to a realisation that: 'Hell! We're the minder. She's the one who is developing him!' Because we just have him for an hour in the morning and an hour at night during the week. And so if I'm feeling low that bothers me ... And I wish it was me who was doing it. But otherwise I just don't think about it because he doesn't come to any harm. So I accept that ... that we haven't got a child full-time and that's it.
>
> (*Local government administrator, aged 35*)

Ways of relieving the tension

When life begins to get on top of them some women experience 'pent up' feelings which they need to discharge. The resulting outburst often relieves the tension. If it occurs in someone else's presence a sympathetic response can help.

> The feeling that everything was getting on top of me, of everything coming up together ... just suddenly feeling I'd got a lot on my plate – having the baby to look after, having to go back to work, having to sell the house and move out of London ... I'm a born worrier really ... I sort of know I can cope but every now and again I need a bit of sympathy ... Yes, I get depressed. It's really just a burst of tears that helps.
>
> (*Careers officer, aged 34*)

Angry outbursts sometimes produce quite the opposite of what women require. A more successful way of dealing with negative feelings is to confide the *problem* rather than just the angry feeling to someone else, particularly to a person in 'the same boat' as oneself. About half of the women say they try to do this. Many more would like opportunities to unburden themselves. (They often asked us how other women taking part in the study were faring and more than one suggested that we should put the women in the study in contact with one another.)

Women experience other negative feelings on their return to work

– tiredness, tension and irritability (see Chapter 7). They resort to a number of ways of alleviating these negative feelings. In an attempt to relax after their children are in bed some resort to alcohol; one woman uses sweets as her 'magic restorative'. A few say they have put themselves on courses of vitamin tablets in order to gain more energy.

Women's ways of managing their return to work highlight the need to be self reliant. In other words women largely cope on their own and take most of the responsibility upon themselves. There are of course notable exceptions where women clearly depend on the support of another person. Husbands' support, as we describe in Chapter 9, is in general somewhat limited. Although some provide considerable back up help they tend to be more valued for their moral and emotional support. On a routine day-to-day basis women manage as best they can by drawing on their own resources which are principally practical and psychological.

Crisis situations are more likely than routine, everyday life to put resources and support to the test. As well as disturbing the order of our lives they are likely to upset us emotionally to the extent that they require additional resources – usually in the form of help from others. Typical crises women experience are children being ill or the breakdown of the childcare arrangement (some of these are described in Chapter 6). Other unrelated crises also occur – deaths and illness among kin and friends, for example. It would therefore be facile to attribute all the stress and distress women experience around the time of their return to work to the tensions of combining parenthood and employment. In the reality of people's lives the picture is more complicated. Here we have focused upon the typical coping strategies women employ in combining motherhood with full-time employment.

CHAPTER 9

Husbands and fathers

> He gets her up in the morning and plays with her for five to ten minutes, which he never used to do. (*Since you went back?*) Yes, that is quite a big change. He does more, purely because I ask him to do things. Before I didn't have to ask him, because I didn't need to (have the help). Nothing is spontaneous . . . A bit more spontaneity would be nice. (*How far do you feel he understands what it's like being a working mother?*) I think he's very factual in attitude. It was discussed, if we have a baby I have to go back to work – therefore you knew what it was going to entail, so you can't really moan. If I try and discuss things that the baby's done and I say 'I wish I'd been there', it's very much brushed aside. It's almost as if it were your decision to have the baby.
>
> (*Education welfare officer, aged 29*)

THE DIVISION OF LABOUR

Fathers in dual earner households contribute to housework and childcare, but not on an equal basis. Their contribution is essentially secondary.

Women's accounts show that not only do most men generally do less work than their wives, but they rarely assume *responsibility* for the work. They adopt the role of helper or assistant, not of equal partner. Often, husbands have to be asked to do things. They fail to see what needs doing, or see but don't do anything about it.

> I'm not happy with the housework. Not so much how to get it done, I can get it done (but) the whole thing boils down to – the running of the house is down to me. OK, he'll cook, but he wouldn't think, is there anything to cook? OK, he'll put the washing on, but he wouldn't think has the baby something to wear tomorrow? It's basically down to the management of it, although he does share the work.
>
> (*Teacher, aged 26*)

Women may not have to do all the work themselves; but they often feel that it is ultimately down to them to ensure that it all gets done.

The search for childcare

Women take on the main burden of searching for childcare, as has been described in Chapter 4. A small number of childcare arrangements are made jointly by both parents and even fewer by fathers alone: but the great majority are made wholly or mainly by mothers.

Though mothers do most of the work, fathers usually make some contribution. Very few women say their husbands take absolutely no part. The most common contribution is discussion, though the extent of this varies. Some men take part in the detailed consideration of the available options.

> I had to make a decision. My husband and I talked it over and tried to make a list of the pluses and minuses . . . I think in the end he just wanted me to do what I felt happiest with.
>
> (*Librarian, aged 34*)

Two interesting points about this example are how the mother defines the situation – '*I* had to make a decision'; and how the father, despite his involvement in the review of options, distances himself from the final decision – 'He wanted me to do what I felt happiest with'.

Generally fathers do not get involved in detailed discussion of options. More often, their role is to 'rubber stamp' decisions made by their wives. Only a third of mothers describe their husbands as 'equally involved' in making the final decision on childcare (and to avoid confusion, it is possible to be 'equally involved' in a decision, without doing the work). Most women say that they make the final decision, usually after some discussion with their husband, though in a few cases without any discussion at all.

If most fathers discuss childcare, however minimally, only a minority take any practical part in making the arrangement. This minority of course includes the few fathers who take the lead in making the arrangement. A few men contribute practically by providing care themselves for part of the time, an offer which may involve rearranging their hours of work. In other cases, fathers participate actively in the search for childcare.

> He phoned the minders. I gave him the questions and he asked them, (though) I think if I hadn't suggested him phoning up various places, he wouldn't have done it.
>
> (*Bank secretary, aged 28*)

The most common practical contribution is to visit a proposed placement, once located by the mother.

> He was very keen to be involved (in making the childcare arrangement), but he kept saying it was my decision ... (Eventually the mother found a childminder, about whom she was) quite happy, but I wanted a second opinion. He didn't visit until the night before Ann was due to start ... (but) I was reassured once he'd been.
>
> (*Librarian, aged 33*)

Domestic work

When a woman goes back to work, it might seem likely that she and her husband would discuss and plan the division of the housework. In practice, this rarely happens. Many couples – about half – do not discuss the subject at all or, in a few cases, they discuss but reach no conclusion. Around a quarter discuss the situation and agree how certain jobs are to be allocated. However, they rarely discuss the complete workload: the focus is often limited to particular crisis times and is more often about childcare than housework. The discussion rarely produces a fair allocation of work overall. Lorraine, a nurse, for instance, has to work a shift which involves two evenings a week, and she and her husband discuss and arrange how their daughter will be cared for on those evenings.

> My husband knew he'd have to pick Jo up and change her and feed her and get her ready for bed and all that. Before (I went) back to work, he learned what had to be done for her in the evening. (*So you said in the evenings you'll do this and that*?) That's right.
>
> (*Ward sister, aged 28*)

In another household, the critical time in the day is the early morning. Janet lives in the country, an hour and a half's journey from her job in a central London hospital. She travels to work together with her husband and young daughter, who goes to a creche at the hospital. The long journey requires an early start.

> I suppose we discussed it ... yes, we did have quite a strict routine, especially in the morning. His main routine of helping was in the morning – he used to prepare Elizabeth's drink and it was ready for me to take. Now he gets her breakfast ready ... we (made arrangements) for the morning – we don't plan the evenings quite so.
>
> (*Senior laboratory technician, aged 34*)

For about another quarter of couples, discussion leads to a general, and usually very vague, understanding that the husband will do more in the home, a statement of good intent rather than a practical plan of action.

> (It was discussed) in a fairly flippant way. We didn't have very serious discussion. (*Was a routine agreed*?) No. I think it was just generally accepted that he would help with the baby. But he was quite adamant he wouldn't do the ironing. But should I ask him to do anything, he'd chip in. There was no 'I'll definitely do this, you'll definitely do that'.
>
> (*Education welfare officer, aged 29*)

Once they have resumed work, many women – rather over a half – report an increase in the amount of domestic work their husbands do. Despite this, employed mothers still do well over half the housework and childcare (see Table 9.1). Over half the fathers do routine individual childcare jobs (such as feeding, changing nappies) less often than 'most days', though nearly all fathers manage to find time to play with their children most days or every day. A majority of children who wake in the night are mostly or always seen to by mothers, while for the rest, the work is usually shared. Only rarely do fathers get up more often than mothers.

For housework, fathers are most likely to clear up after meals, followed by shopping and cooking, and least likely to do cleaning – either of clothes or the house – or ironing (see Table 9.2).

Childcare arrangements

Even where both parents have full-time jobs, fathers are usually out at work (including travel time) longer than mothers, around an hour a day more on average (the average working week for men with young children, including overtime, second jobs and journeys is 50 to 55 hours). Consequently, mothers spend more time with their children each day. In some cases, though, fathers do care for their children for part of the time that mothers are at work. The extent of this contribution varies considerably – an occasional evening or weekend, during school holidays (for some fathers who are teachers), half an hour or an hour each day, through to a few fathers whose contribution is really substantial, more than 10 hours a week.

Often, this is made possible because the father or mother works shifts. Jessica, a 22 year old bank clerk, for instance, works a regular nine to five day in the City, while John, her husband, works a double day shift – 6 am to 1.30 pm one week, 1.30–9 pm the next – as a tool setter at a factory near their home. When John is on 'earlies', Jessica takes their son to the childminder on her way to work and John collects him just after 1.30, on his way home from work. When on 'lates', the routine is reversed so that John cares for their son at home in the morning, and takes him to the childminder's on his way to work at 1.15, leaving Jessica to collect him on her way home.

In another instance, the father, Jeff, changed his hours of work at the Post Office to permanent nights specifically to ensure that his daughter will not have to spend all day at a childminder's when his wife resumes work. The mother, Maureen, a 28 year old bank clerk, takes the baby to the childminder's on her way in to work, collects her again at lunch, takes her home and puts her down to sleep. At this stage of the day, both the young child and her father are asleep at home. The child wakes later in the afternoon, and Jeff then gets up and cares for his daughter until Maureen gets home from work.

Despite these examples, most fathers are not involved in the care of their children while mothers are working. Nor are most fathers involved with the childminders, relatives or nurseries who provide the main childcare arrangements. Usually children are taken and collected by mothers. And because of this, it is mainly mothers who 'service' the arrangements, giving such time and thought as is necessary to keep them working smoothly.

HOW MOTHERS FEEL ABOUT THEIR HUSBAND'S CONTRIBUTION

Few women are critical of their husband's part in the search for childcare – criticism here is much more likely to be levelled at formal services. Criticism of husbands' contribution to the domestic workload is more common, but is still raised by only a minority of women – just over a third. Such criticism as there is tends to be about specific issues and areas, rather than blanket disapproval of what husbands do, or don't do. Some women approve of what their partners do in one area, but not another. A common pattern is for men to do more childcare than housework, and this can draw criticism.

> I get enough help with Jo . . . (on housework) when it comes to basics, for instance hoovering, if I ask him, he'll do it, but I don't like to have to ask him, I'd prefer that he did it . . . with the house, if you want me to speak honestly, I'd like more (contribution from husband).
>
> (*Senior bank clerk, aged 27*)

It might seem surprising that employed women are not more critical of their husbands. Moreover, much of the criticism is muted, qualified or only emerges after considerable probing. Why should this be so?

Undoubtedly, a small proportion of women still explicitly believe that women *should* do more housework and childcare, even if both parents have full-time jobs. For instance, Pauline, a 30 year old clerical assistant, says work should be equally divided 'except where things are not suitable for men to do – washing or ironing is not really a man's job'. While Lorraine, a ward sister aged 28, feels the work should not be divided right down the middle, because 'it's nice if the wife can do a little bit more and make her husband a little bit proud of her because she does the house'. Some women also believe that men cannot be expected to take the initiative in housework.

> Since I've been back to work, he's had to do a little bit more – hoovering, getting James ready for bed and when I'm home late, he gets the tea ... it's just a case of asking, 'Will you do A and B?' I don't think men like to be told, you'll be doing such-and-such a thing. I think it's better if you say 'Would you do this?'
>
> (*Clerical assistant, aged 30*)

WHY WOMEN ACCEPT THE SITUATION

Mostly working mothers, certainly those in full-time jobs, do subscribe to 'equal shares' – at least in principle. The commitment is, however, often not very deep-rooted: in opinion poll jargon, support for 'equal shares' is decidedly soft. A contributory reason is men's perceived or actual incompetence domestically – 'He made such a hash of most jobs, I'd rather do it myself'.

More significant, and nearer the heart of the matter, is that many women still see their own employment as secondary to their husbands'. Many women, just over half, say that even from their *own* point of view, their own work is less important than their husband's; while even more consider the husband's job as more important from the *household's* point of view, because his pay and prospects are better. Many women expect to leave employment at some point in the future, usually when their second child is born. These two views do not necessarily go together – some women may, for instance, expect to continue working without a break, yet still consider their husband's work more important. But these views lead women to accept that their husband has the lead role in the household when it comes to paid work; and that they should therefore assume the lead role in domestic work. Each woman tends to feel that this is the best practical solution in her own case rather than a reflection of current ideology.

This position is reinforced by other pressures. Most women who return to their job after maternity leave see it as 'their' choice to go back to work, not as part of a joint decision about the organisation of paid work. They therefore regard it as down to them to manage the consequences of their 'choice'.

Women who do resume work have to cope with the widely held beliefs that women with young children should not go out to work, and that the 'good mother' is primarily responsible for home and child. Such beliefs may be rejected or questioned at a rational level, but they still exert a powerful influence on how women feel and make them vulnerable to guilt about what they do for their children and about standards of housework. Such beliefs about women's roles are disseminated and reinforced by clear and frequent messages – in the media and elsewhere – about how the 'good' mother *should* behave. Working mothers are regularly confronted by these powerful messages – not by alternative messages about the behaviour of women and men who subscribe to more egalitarian beliefs. Women are likely to know very few, if any, men – either through media images or personally – who in their attitudes and behaviour provide a model of an equally participant husband. The only standard against which women can generally assess their husband's contribution is 'most men'. Judged against this low standard of participation, working mothers are on the whole likely to feel that their husbands perform adequately or even relatively well.

In such circumstances, it is hardly surprising that many women do not criticise their husbands' contribution to housework or to making childcare arrangements, or else that they are restrained or hesitant in their criticism. To be ambivalent and doubtful about your own actions is not a firm basis on which to question and challenge the actions of others.

GOING BACK TO WORK – FATHERS' VIEWS

Women's experience of going back to work after maternity leave can be influenced by their husbands in several ways. Their practical support in the search for childcare and the domestic workload has already been considered. Their attitude to their wife's decision to resume employment is also important. Support in this matter provides legitimation and backing to a woman in a society where her decision to return to employment is unusual and widely criticised. Opposition from the husband will make employment more difficult, both emotionally and practically: indeed, strong and sustained opposition may make it virtually impossible for a woman to remain at work.

At one end of the spectrum some husbands do express open disapproval.

> He thinks I'm the only one who should look after the child – nobody else should. We do discuss (my return) but it usually ends in arguments. He throws at me that I shouldn't have had a child if I wanted to go back to work.
>
> (*Teacher, aged 26*)

At the other extreme, some men are unreservedly in favour of their wives working.

> He's very supportive of what I want to do. But I think he sees it as my decision. But I think he'd want me to go back anyway. Again, it's something we've talked about over a long period.
>
> (*Senior local government officer, aged 29*)

In between these extremes come the majority of husbands. Their views – at least as perceived by their wives – are not so clear-cut. Some men prefer, or are thought to prefer, their wives to work, but hedge this with qualifications, for instance wishing their wives could work shorter hours or do otherwise less demanding jobs. Other men would in principle prefer their wives to be at home, but accept the need for work, often because they acknowledge that the household needs two incomes, at least for a time.

> I have to go back but mainly for financial reasons ... as he put it, what would we rather have – I go back to work and get some money behind us to give Alison a good start or (be) like some unfortunate people, try and struggle and end up rowing ... he'd like me to say at work 'Thank you, I'm off', (but) as much as he'd like me to be at home, we both know it's not going to be.
>
> (*Clerical assistant, aged 30*)

Other men recognise that their wives need to work, but for their own well-being.

> I suppose by the way he was brought up, like most men he'd like me to be at home. But he knows what I feel, he knows I

> wouldn't be happy ... he's never said 'I don't want you to go back'.
>
> (*Bank clerk, aged 26*)

Yet another variant is for men to prefer their wives to be at home, but to take a public position that 'of course, it's entirely up to you'.

> He's taken it for granted I'll go back. He's said it's up to me, do what I want to do. (But) I think he'd really like me to stay at home and look after her.
>
> (*Teacher, aged 30*)

In some cases, where husbands take this line – 'it's up to you' – women are left uncertain about what their husbands really do think.

> I think he wants me to go back, in that it'll make him feel more stable because his work (as a building worker) is so irregular ... I'm not going to say he'd ideally want me to go full-time, but some sort of work, so if he wasn't working we'd have something to fall back on. He left it up to me ... I don't think he has a preference, I think he really says it's up to me.
>
> (*Senior bank clerk, aged 27*)

This leaves a final group of husbands who express no opinion or view at all, perhaps to avoid giving offence or because they genuinely are uncertain what they feel.

Husband's views on the issue are therefore seldom simply 'for' or 'against'. The situation is usually much less straightforward. Husband's positions are often characterised by uncertainty, qualifications and contradictory attitudes and feelings. One consequence is that women often receive mixed messages from their husbands – they rarely get unqualified and total approval.

Sometimes the contradictions in a man's position are presented clearly – for instance, 'I'd rather you were at home but I accept you should work for now because we need the money'. Whether this is helpful or unhelpful for his wife will vary. At least, though, she is likely to understand her husband's position.

In other cases though, the message is far more ambivalent, with the contradictions not fully resolved.

> He said he didn't really want me to go back to work, but there's no choice. I think in an ideal world, he thinks women should be at home. I think he used to think that, but as it's come on, I think he thinks women should return if they want to – and I have to . . . he says, 'Women should stay at home' and then I say 'Right, I'll stay at home' and he says 'No! we need the money'.
>
> (*Social worker, aged 30*)

A more subtle example is provided by Pat. She is an NHS audiology technician, a job she has done for five years. Her husband, James, is 27, a sales representative for health products, but out of work for four months when Pat returns to work. Before her return, she describes some ambivalence in James' position.

> (He says) it's entirely up to you, because I'm a person in my own right. I'm as much a partnership as he is, it's purely up to me . . . (but) like most fathers he'd like to think I'd be a mother to his child and be with his child. In some respects he'd like me to give up.
>
> (*Audiology technician, aged 24*)

In the interview, after Pat had been back at work for some months, she starts by describing James' position as genuinely and unreservedly open-minded.

> He's one of those people who are middle of the road. He wouldn't mind one way or the other, he didn't prefer me to stay at home or work. It's entirely as long as I'm happy.

Elsewhere, however, reservations emerge. James' position becomes less clear, the message he is sending Pat more ambivalent and less supportive.

> He doesn't mind me working, he doesn't mind that aspect of it, it's just purely I'm getting tired at the end of the day. Therefore I'm not giving the benefit to the family, the benefit is going to the work and that's what he's opposed to . . . He says it's entirely up to me (but) looking at it from his point of view, he'd prefer it if I wasn't working or if I wasn't as tired.

A sense of understanding

To feel that your situation and experience is appreciated by others, especially those to whom you feel close, may be an important source of support, especially during demanding periods in life. Just under a half of the women say, without qualification, that their husbands are understanding about what it is like to be a working mother with a young baby and what that involves. The remaining husbands are considered either understanding in some ways but not in others, or as not being understanding at all. Husbands are felt to lack understanding in two main respects. First, they fail to comprehend the amount and complexity of work involved in responsibility for running a home and caring for a baby.

> I don't think he appreciates fully everything I have to do and think about, and the forward planning ... like getting everything ready for Jo. He thinks it's a matter of just walking out of the house – he doesn't stop to think she needs nappies, food. He wonders why it takes so long. He doesn't realise the planning and thinking.
>
> (*Senior bank clerk, aged 27*)

Second, they show a lack of understanding about women's feelings. The most common example arises over women's guilt about working and leaving children.

> He understands from a practical point of view how much work is involved, but I don't think he understands the emotional, wanting to be with Gill. He's a bit baffled because he's better at switching off after leaving the house.
>
> (*Personal assistant, aged 30*)

> I have discussed my guilt to some extent. He sympathises, but says I'm making mountains out of molehills ... he tries to understand. His argument is that nobody ever expects a father to stay at home with a baby, so why should I feel I'm any more deprived than anyone else.
>
> (*Executive officer in the civil service, aged 32*)

Some husbands do not appear to understand how tired their wives feel.

> I don't think men do (understand). Sorry about that! (to male interviewer). There's a lot to do with stereotyping mothers. They look at their own mother (and think) they can manage, why can't you. I suppose he just feels – he can't see my tiredness is more than his. This is our argument all the time – 'I'm more tired than you', 'Why should you be?' He doesn't understand there's more to it than that, just being more aware of her needs.
> (*Teacher, aged 30*)

Some of the instances in which husbands appear to show a lack of understanding, in particular through denying or minimising problems and feelings, may result from inappropriate attempts to help. Most often, though, men fail to recognise and understand the differences in experience and feelings of working mothers and fathers. Mothers carry the greater load of domestic work and responsibility; they are exposed to a climate of disapproval for working; and they resume their jobs after a prolonged period at home with their child. Resuming work means a major change in the circumstances of their parenting, as well as having to 'leave' their child. None of this is so for fathers whose working patterns and lives remain unchanged.

Three fathers

Contributions made by husbands do not fall into neat categories: instead, there is a range of participation and support. The three fathers described below represent different points on the spectrum. George contributes very little in any way; indeed in some ways, he makes life harder for his wife. Alan, by contrast, is in virtually every way equally participant and wholly supportive. George and Alan represent extreme positions on the continuum, occupied by relatively small proportions of fathers, around 1 in 10 in each case. The great majority of fathers come somewhere between. Gordon, the third father described here, represents a midway point.

GEORGE

George is 28 and a finance officer; his wife, Deborah, is 23 and a clerical worker in a government department. They had been married for two years when their daughter, Maria, was born. Deborah went back to work when Maria was seven months old – but reluctantly, under pressure from George.

> My husband has (made up his mind). I knew as well that financially there was no question (of not returning). It's always been there, but I pushed it to the back of my mind ... about a month ago when my husband knew he'd be changing job and get a rise in salary, we talked about whether I could give up work and at one point he said yes – but then a few days later he changed and put it down on paper, that it would be an existence rather than living. I was blackmailed by him saying that Maria wouldn't be able to have this, that or the other. He'd like me to stay at home. But he's more practical than I am, so although he thinks it's nice for the mother to stay at home, he looks at it from another point of view ... (his attitude was) basically unhelpful. I know what his opinion is, so really discussions we've had have just been for the sake of it.

Deborah's mother offered to care for Maria, so making childcare arrangements involved little work. Maria is taken and collected by George and Deborah, who drive to and from work together. George did 'very little' in the house before Deborah resumed work, and does little more now she is back.

> He's a little better than he was, since I was back at work. I suppose he is. Mainly the hoovering – but I'm not sure if that's because we've bought a new hoover and he enjoys using it or thinks 'I'll help her out'. He deals with the baby's bottles, he washes them out, but he did that before I went back. Occasionally he'll wash up in the evening, which he never did before.

The only jobs George does as often as once a week are shopping and bathing Maria. Particularly demanding in this household is the work created by Maria's frequent night-waking.

> Since two months before I went back to work, we've had murder with her. She won't go off to sleep without a screaming fit and she wakes four or five times a night ... I get very tired ... I get home from work, cook the tea and that's it – I don't feel like doing anything.

George never puts Maria to bed or gets up to her – nor does he ever make the tea, despite the fact he and Deborah get home together.

Deborah does not believe that housework and childcare should be equally shared: 'I suppose 60/40, the woman should obviously take the most of it'. She explains this view in personal terms.

> Because he works harder at work. There is more mental fatigue. And I suppose in a way I like to do it myself because I'm never happy with the way he does it.

Related to this, Deborah finds it difficult to ask for help.

> It's really when I feel I'm at the end of my tether, that if he doesn't do something soon I'm going to snap – then I'll ask. I'll ask him to run downstairs and get me a nappy, or run upstairs and get me this or that, which he usually does. I wouldn't think for an instant of asking him to feed the baby. I suppose I tend to think that's my role – I'm the mother. And I just know he wouldn't be enjoying it.

She does make some criticisms, although her low expectations make them quite restrained.

> He's helped more, to a degree – but not as much as I'd like. I just feel sometimes (I'd like him to) take her off me, to say 'You get on with what you're doing, I'll look after the baby for half an hour', so I could do something else like wash the floor . . . at the moment I feel the baby is a permanent attachment. I don't mind the housework as long as he'll remove her.

George shows little understanding of Deborah's feelings. She is unhappy being at work and remains very guilty about not caring for Maria – 'I feel somehow that you're deserting your baby'.

> Sometimes I think he understands, but at other times he's inconsiderate, and doesn't seem to realise at all what I'm doing. I think he doesn't think of my job as work, he thinks it's all a big laugh . . . he's sympathetic (about my guilt feelings) but I think he thinks I'm inventing things to worry about . . . I don't think he considers it's a worry. It wouldn't worry him.

GORDON

Gordon is 31 and a secondary school teacher. As well as basic school hours, he brings work home regularly to do in the evenings and at weekends. Caroline is 29, and a solicitor working in a local authority. They had been married a year before the birth of Stephen, but had lived together for eight years before that.

Caroline found Gordon supportive when making her decision to go back to work, even though she perceives his attitude as one of only qualified approval.

> He thinks it's a good idea to go back ... I think he thinks it's quite a good idea to go back for the stimulation. At his school, quite a lot of the women go back and enjoy it ... (*Helpful*?) It's very good in the sense we've decided I'm going back and therefore it's very positive ... I think he'd like me to return (though) he'd probably feel it was better if I could work part-time.

After considering a nursery for Stephen (the parents are highly unusual in that both have employers with some workplace nursery provision), it was arranged that Stephen would be looked after by the wife of Gordon's brother. Caroline however actually made the arrangement and once back at work, takes and collects Stephen.

Before Caroline resumed work, she did 'most of the everyday care' for Stephen. Gordon was 'very good at playing and giving time and attention'.

> He's very good on the whole, particularly in the first few weeks when (Stephen) cried a lot and needed a lot of holding and comforting. He's a good support ... (though) every so often I think he could do something (more) – but no more than that.

Caroline resumed work when Stephen was six months old. She describes Gordon's contribution to domestic tasks as increasing but 'not a lot – he tries to help where and when he can'. His work continues to make demands, after school and at weekends.

> He has to do some work at home. The nights he doesn't work at home at least he helps me and it just makes it a lot easier. But he has to do his work. Usually he comes in and works as soon as he

> gets home. When I come in, I'll deal with Stephen, get tea, get him bathed. If he's working on the domestic front then, it makes the whole evening run more smoothly. It'd be lovely if he didn't have to do as much work at home ... (but) if you are a conscientious teacher, you have to do marking ... if he was going to help equally with me he'd probably end up marking books at midnight.

Caroline does most of the childcare and housework tasks, but at least once a week George does each of the childcare tasks, and also cooks and cleans the house regularly. Perhaps most important, he cares for Stephen during most of the school holidays.

Caroline is still critical of his contribution to domestic work, though her criticisms remain heavily qualified, reflecting a basic ambivalence.

> I'd love more help, but I don't think it's particularly practicable. He looks after the car, does more of the garden (the garden was minute). But he does fit in more leisure-time ... he's very good at playing with Stephen. I suppose he could change more nappies and what have you. It doesn't get me down he doesn't do more – (but) he could help a bit more I suppose.

Caroline feels Gordon is understanding of what it's like to be a working mother – but with some reservations.

> I think in general (he's understanding) ... but I don't think he's always ... things like in the morning he goes off before I do and I don't think he's got an idea of how much I have to rush around to get out.

ALAN

Alan is 29 and a social worker. He usually works a regular nine to five day. Margaret is 28 and a teacher-instructor in a social education centre for people with mental handicaps. When Sophie was born, they were not married but had lived together for five years.

Margaret found Alan extremely supportive of her decision to continue at work.

> He thought it was important, if that was my choice, if I wanted to. He knew I would find it difficult to cope at home all day, just me and the baby. (*Was he helpful?*) Extremely ... he made me weigh up the situation, look at it from the point of view of 'what did I want'.

Sophie went to a childminder. Margaret made the arrangement, but Alan was very involved in the decision, in a way that Margaret again found very supportive.

> He stressed it really was important that I felt happy with the childminder because it really was my decision again, even though it was shared (for) if I wasn't happy with the childminder it would be ridiculous. He pointed out a few things to think about when choosing her ... very practical things, but he also said, which struck me as very interesting, how would I get on with the childminder, how would I feel as a mother giving my child to somebody, trying to live that action ... also we talked in great depth about preparing, taking Sophie beforehand, for us to get to know the childminder.

While Margaret was still on leave, Alan was very participant in all childcare tasks – '(he gives) 100 per cent to all of them even though he is working'.

Margaret resumed her work when Sophie was eight months. Beforehand, the couple had a general discussion about sharing the domestic work, which led to a vague agreement. With Margaret back at work, Alan does at least half the childcare and housework, doing all childcare tasks daily and all housework tasks (except ironing, which neither do) at least weekly. Margaret is very positive about both his practical contribution and his emotional support.

> He's so totally involved, he knows exactly what it's like. He's more understanding than most men I know ... he said I had become so inward-looking while I was at home that he wanted me to go back and now he says it was definitely the right thing to do.

When Sophie was three years old, Margaret talked further about Alan's involvement. This provides a still clearer picture of what it means to be an equally participant father in a dual earner household, and is a suitable note on which to conclude this chapter – looking at what is possible, rather than at what still predominates.

> There was no pressure (that) I had to work. It was 'What do you want to do?' He was advising me, saying, 'Look, you're obviously not happy, what do you want to do?' then he supported me in whatever decision I made. Once I'd let go of Sophie, his relationship with her began to develop, which was healthy for us all ... when I started to work, the first three months I was eaten up with guilt... (then) I'd come home from work and he'd collected her from the childminder's and was feeding her and managing beautifully. And it suddenly dawned on me that I wasn't the only person who could look after her. Because both of us work, we need an afternoon or a morning of the weekend to ourselves ... one of us will have the morning, the other the afternoon. I say to him sometimes, 'Right, you're going out this afternoon!' I sometimes worry I'm putting too much on him. Because after all I'm a woman and what is this total shared care of the child. It's unusual ... (but) I feel he's very proud we have a kind of lifestyle he'd have wanted ... he thinks it's hard, but it's fruitful, it's exciting. I'd say the responsibility (for Sophie's care and upbringing) is shared between us. (*Down the middle*?) I think it is. (*Who would take her to the doctor's*?) I do or him, it depends on what we are doing. (*Who would stay at home if Sophie was ill*?) Either – or sometimes both. Childcare has got to be shared. (*Can men do it as well as women*?) Yes, and maybe better because the relationship is very different between father and child. He stands back. I give in to her, he doesn't. The joke is that she wants to get back into the womb, and I mean it's just very apparent, she just wants me, she's very clingy. And she's not like that with him. That's why I admire men who have good relationships with their children, who participate, share the responsibility, because they are giving a different sort of relationship.

CHAPTER 10

Where next?

The accounts of women who resume employment after maternity leave include much that is positive. The great majority feel they have made the right decision. Most feel they are coping adequately, both at home and at work. Once they are back at their jobs, most feel far less guilty and anxious than beforehand. Most women consider their childcare arrangements work at least adequately, and that their children gain from being cared for by others for part of the time. There is sufficient here to reassure and encourage women who are considering whether or not to go back to their jobs after having a child.

The situation though is not perfect – far from it. The evidence from our study and other studies, and from other countries where far more women with young children are in employment, is that many mothers in Britain would like to continue in employment, but are deterred from so doing in present circumstances. Many women who do resume employment when they have young children are forced to take poor jobs, below the level at which they previously worked, often doing marginal work, involving very short hours, low pay and no opportunities for advancement.

The relatively few women, such as those in our study, who resume their former jobs on a full-time basis face other problems. There is little flexibility about the basis on which they work: in most cases, they must return immediately on a full-time basis. They experience a high level of guilt and anxiety before they go back: once back at work, these feelings can and do recur. They carry a heavy workload – a full-time job, finding and maintaining the childcare arrangement, doing most of the housework and childcare and carrying most of the responsibility. As well as coping with this heavy routine workload, occasional and often unpredictable demands have to be accommodated – a sick child, a visit to the doctor or the clinic, out-of-hours work meetings. Women show great skill and resources in coping with these various demands, but they can often lead to feelings of pressure, tension and tiredness.

Choice in childcare is limited: in particular, there is little nursery provision available for young children, despite many mothers being interested in this type of care. A substantial minority of childcare arrangements either fail and need to be changed, or create other difficulties. By the time they have been back at work for several months, however, most women are satisfied with their arrangements, and feel their children benefit from others being involved in their care – though there are problems in deciding the significance of such satisfaction in a context where alternatives are often limited, and the very act of leaving a child in someone else's care causes so much anxiety and guilt. In general, little work has been done on the quality of childcare services in Britain. Such as there is, mostly about childminding, suggests that standards vary greatly, with substantial pockets of poor quality, which children from economically disadvantaged homes are most likely to receive. Overall, our study suggests that care by relatives is least problematic for parents, but we have no evidence at this point in our study, or from other studies, about the quality of care provided.

There is an additional problem. Many of those who care for the children of working parents receive poor pay and work in difficult conditions. A childminder looking after three children for 40 hours a week at the rate recommended by the National Childminders Association (£27 per child) would have an income of less than £1.75 an hour *before* expenses, insurance, tax, and so on. A 'living out' nanny, outside London, might be paid £70 a week (the rate suggested in the *Working Mothers Handbook* – see Appendix 3). The salary for a qualified nursery nurse in her first job in a council day nursery varies between local authorities, but will usually be between £100 and £110 a week; on average in private nurseries the pay is probably somewhat lower. By comparison, the average weekly pay for women in non-manual jobs is £134, while for men it is £225. (All figures are for gross weekly pay and refer to 1986–7.)

Lack of alternative jobs ensures that for the moment there are many women prepared to provide childcare under these conditions.

Moreover, while some parents could pay more for childcare, many already find the cost a substantial burden, especially as the cost is often regarded as a charge to be set against the mother's earnings only, rather than a charge on total household earnings. Childcare provision for employed parents therefore either depends on relatives, a type of care not generally available, nor generally wanted; or on groups of devalued and exploited workers, whose poor pay and conditions of employment are unsatisfactory in their own right, and not conducive to producing high standards of care.

Finally, it is striking the extent to which women see their decision to go out to work as their personal choice. It is not regarded as a joint decision made by couples as part of a wider discussion about the allocation of all aspects of work, both inside and outside the household. Instead, the continuing employment of fathers is taken for granted, while the mother's is viewed as *her* decision, the consequences as *her* responsibility and problem. Difficulties experienced are often internalised as personal failings rather than a consequence of an unsupportive social context. This perspective contributes to women having high expectations of themselves, and low expectations of others – employers, Government, husbands, caregivers. Not only do they carry a heavy workload, with relatively little support, but they often accept this as a price they must pay for their course of action.

WHO CAN MAKE CHANGES?

Given present circumstances, there are some steps that women themselves can take which may help, either when it comes to deciding whether to resume employment after childbirth or on actually going back. Talking to other women who are in the same situation, and to those who have been back for some time, can be particularly valuable, for providing reassurance, moral and emotional support and practical advice. Reading the experiences of others, such as those in this book, may also help. There are a number of useful organisations and publications, some of which are included at the back of the book.

It would however be inappropriate to place too much emphasis on what women themselves need to do. Women already make enormous efforts to cope in a social context that is harsh and unsupportive. It is here that the main changes need to occur. A change in attitudes and behaviour needs to be set in train, that will create a social context that is supportive to working mothers. The process of change involves several key groups: fathers, employers and government.

Fathers

Some fathers already take a genuinely equal part in childcare and other domestic responsibilities. They are though still a very small minority. Most men have a long way to go, both in what they actually do and in the level of responsibility they assume. It is not, however, purely a matter of individual will and commitment. There are also powerful constraints on how men think and behave: change in how fathers act is to some extent also dependent on changes in the social context.

Employers

Employers, for instance, can play a major role in creating a more supportive context for both women and men. This can be done in several ways. Employment practices can be reviewed, introducing for instance new leave entitlements and more flexible and varied working hours. Employers can contribute to childcare, by making their own provision, buying places in outside services or by contributing to employees' costs. They can set up refresher courses for women returning from maternity leave. They can invest in training and other ways of increasing understanding and support between managers and staff with children and other dependants. The workplace can also provide opportunities for women and men to discuss issues that arise from combining employment and parenthood, for instance through staff in personnel departments, through organising small groups of workers in similar circumstances or by linking workers who have young children with those who are anticipating parenthood.

Such employer initiatives should be concerned not just with women, but with *all* employees who have, or anticipate having, children. There has long been an argument that special measures for women or, more specifically for mothers, will deter employers from recruiting women. We remain to be convinced by this argument:

introduction of maternity leave, for instance, appears to have had no such impact. It is, however, beside the point. Measures concerned with parenthood should be seen as needed by and applicable to both men and women.

Some employers have already gone a considerable way towards recognising the needs of employees with children. The most substantial changes have occurred in the public sector, particularly among the relatively small number of local authorities with a strong commitment to equal opportunities. Innovations in the private sector have been less common, and in some cases, as with the major banks, have been confined to women in a limited range of high status jobs. Overall, most employers have done little or nothing, a situation encouraged by the low priority given to these matters by many Trade Unions. Experience therefore suggests that to rely on employer initiatives, and on voluntary agreements between employers and employees, will produce progress that is slow and uneven, missing many workers, especially those in the least skilled or poorest paid jobs.

Government

This is one reason why, in our view, the process of change must involve intervention by society as a whole, acting through the institutions of government. Current employment patterns and practice, which take so little account of domestic responsibilities, constitute in effect a set of restrictions which favour men who do not carry an equal share of these responsibilities. A society which claims a commitment to equality of opportunity has to challenge such practices *if* it is serious in its commitment.

There are other reasons why government should intervene in the issue of parental employment. Having children and raising them is not merely a private indulgence on the part of parents. It is also an activity of the most major social importance, involving the nurturance, socialisation and development of the next generation, society's most valuable resource. There is, or should be, a bargain involved. Society expects parents to perform an important and demanding job for it. In return it should ensure that parents have sufficient resources for the job, *and* that they are not excluded from participating fully in society or otherwise disadvantaged as a consequence of the work involved.

The bargain should include those who care for children while their parents are at work. These workers, virtually all women, are currently recruited to care for children for very low pay and in very poor conditions. This is a reflection of the unequal position that women occupy in the labour market in our society, not of the value and complexity of the work involved. A solution to the childcare problems faced by employed parents should not be based on the continuing exploitation of this group of workers. Not only is this wrong, and incompatible with any commitment to equality, but it is also unlikely to produce good quality childcare. Experience in other fields, where poor pay and conditions lead to poor performance, applies equally to childcare.

At present, relatives provide a major source of childcare in the UK. They cannot, however, provide a substitute for properly paid childcare workers. Many parents have no relatives living close enough to provide care, and many would in any case not wish to have their children cared for in this way. Moreover the supply of female relatives ready and willing to provide care is limited, and likely to decrease. Employment rates among older women – in the 45 to 60 age group – have risen steadily in the UK, and are now among the highest in Europe. Increasingly, grandmothers and great-aunts – the relatives who provide the great bulk of care at the moment – have jobs, and other interests, that reduce their ability and willingness to look after young children.

Taking all these factors into account, the only way that satisfactory childcare for *all* children can be provided at a price *all* parents can afford, and providing caregivers with pay and conditions that reflect the importance and complexity of their work, is through some degree of government intervention. We would add in conclusion that irrespective of the needs of parents and caregivers, government has an overriding responsibility to ensure the satisfactory care of young children, a particularly weak and powerless section of the community.

WHAT CAN BE DONE

What then might the government do, if it were agreed that it should assume more responsibility? In our view, parental employment and related childcare issues are not private matters to be left to individual parents and employers and the play of market forces. Our government should take responsibility going beyond existing maternity leave legislation and the minimal regulation of childminding and nurseries, as now happens in many other countries.

Raising awareness

First, there is an important educative role to be played, challenging the widespread disapproval of working mothers and the myths that continue to fuel this prejudice; explaining the connections that do exist between parenthood and inequality for women; encouraging discussion of the implications for men of changes in women's position in society; and presenting policy options and their implications. This means giving the issue of parenthood and employment a place, and quite an important one, on the political agenda, where it has not been represented up to now. To the best of our knowledge, no senior politician of any party has ever addressed the issue; there has been no proper debate, let alone regular debates, on the subject in Parliament; and the only official publication of any relevance – *Services for Young Children with Working Mothers* written by the Central Policy Review Staff in 1978 – sank without trace, totally ignored by government. In the circumstances, it is hardly surprising that the level of knowledge and awareness in British society about parenthood and employment is extremely low, or that the public is generally ignorant of the situation in other countries.

Employment practices

Secondly, government can encourage employers to adopt good employment practices. This can be done in several ways. The government, as a major employer, can set an exemplary standard in its own employment practices and policies. It can finance and otherwise support experiments and innovations. It can disseminate the results of these, and set up resource, advice and information services for individuals' employers who want help. It can also provide money and other resources to facilitate change. Finally, it can remove obstacles to employers who wish to provide better facilities for employees with children. In particular, the current tax on parents who use nurseries subsidised by their employers should be scrapped.

Legislation

Thirdly, the government should legislate certain general minimum standards, both to move change along and to protect those employees who work for uninterested or recalcitrant employers. In this respect, four leave entitlements are particular important. *Maternity leave* should be a right available to all employed women, with no qualifying conditions and no exemptions: it should also be made a proper leave, with a clear entitlement to return to the same job. All fathers should be entitled to two weeks *paternity leave*, at the time of their child's birth. Each employee should be entitled to a period of *parental leave*. We would support, as a starting point, the proposal made in the draft Directive prepared by the Commission of the European Economic Community (see Appendix 2), that each employee be entitled to three months leave per child, this leave to be taken at any point between the end of maternity leave and a child's second birthday. We would also support the Directive's proposal of a part-time option, so the leave period could be taken on a part-time basis and extended accordingly – although unlike the EEC Directive, we would favour this part-time option being available as of right (as in Sweden), rather than at the employer's discretion. Finally, parents should be entitled to *leave for family reasons*, guaranteeing each employed parent an annual quota of leave (perhaps 10 days a year per child) to cope with pressing family needs, for instance the care of a sick child, taking a child to medical appointments or settling a child into a new childcare arrangement.

For both parental leave and leave for family reasons, single parents should enjoy a 'double' entitlement, while all leaves should be covered by an earnings-related benefit. No payment or a low flat-rate benefit penalises parents, and acts as a disincentive to taking leave. It also provides an obstactle to fathers taking leave. In present circumstances, where men normally earn more than their partners, there is a strong economic incentive for women to take any leave if it is unpaid or paid at a low flat rate.

Improving childcare

Government's fourth and final role involves assuming responsibility for ensuring a satisfactory level of childcare for all children with working parents. We would also add, though this is less critical, that government should assume responsibility for ensuring parents have some choice of type of childcare. Such a role does not mean that government assumes sole responsibility for childcare, or that it would 'take over' from parents. What it does mean is that government takes a share in childcare, entering into partnership with parents and caregivers, in the same way that it shares in responsibility for children's education and health. The role is that of enabler and guarantor.

To fulfil this role involves some element of funding for services, especially if caregivers are not to be exploited, and are to enjoy the pay and conditions appropriate to the value and demands of the work. Resources also need to be put, on a far larger scale than at present, into monitoring services and improving quality. This leaves many details to be worked out. Who provides the services? How much choice should parents have? Should parents contribute directly to the cost through fees, or indirectly through taxes? Should employers be expected to contribute directly? How can such complex and scattered services be monitored? How can quality be improved? These are important questions, but it is not our task to answer them here. Our concern is limited to proposing the broad principle, that government does have a significant role to play in ensuring an adequate supply of good quality childcare at a price parents can afford.

Possible criticisms

To make proposals such as these courts a number of criticisms. One argument that we have already rejected, is that nothing should be done for working mothers and fathers since mothers should not go out to work and, if they do, they must cope with the consequences. Another criticism might be that these proposals offer relatively simple solutions to complex issues, that they attempt to impose one view on everyone, and that they would be costly and disruptive. We do not treat such views lightly. We do recognise that any process of change is likely to be uncertain, slow and influenced by many factors, many beyond the direct control of government and employers. Change cannot be achieved overnight simply by government action. Much work has to be done in deciding and developing the best policies and services. Having accepted that, we still believe that government and its institutions have a contribution to make to the process of change, limited maybe, but nevertheless important and useful.

In proposing the need for change in the attitudes and behaviour of fathers, especially where their partners are employed, we recognise that many men are reluctant to change. There is also a reluctance or ambivalence among many women about such changes. We are dealing with sensitive issues that touch on important values and feelings. In practice, however, we are talking about a slow and patchy process, involving the development of alternative role models. In the foreseeable future, the most ambitious objective is to encourage real options and genuine plurality: imposing alternatives on reluctant men and women is as impractical as it is undesirable. Similarly, because we advocate the right of women to maintain their attachment to the labour market whilst also becoming mothers, does not mean that we believe all women want to do, or should do, paid work while they have young children. We are concerned with supporting those women who want to follow a particular course of action, not with insisting that that course of action is the only one to be followed.

In conclusion, we would not deny that our proposals – or any proposals to improve the situation of mothers who wish to be employed – involve costs and disruption. Those countries, such as Sweden and Denmark, which have implemented extensive childcare and employment measures to assist parents have managed to absorb such costs and disruption as these measures have involved. Much of the immediate cash cost to government could also be covered by redeploying part of the massive sum currently allocated to the married man's tax allowance, a feature of the taxation system widely regarded as an anachronism.

Furthermore, the existing state of affairs involves its own substantial costs and disruption – for women, children, employers and society at large. So far as we are aware, there has been no attempt to weigh up the costs – or the benefits – of the current situation against the sort of alternative we propose. Such an exercise would be complex. It would need, for instance, to calculate the cost to employers and the economy of losing so many women from the labour force when they have children, then underusing their skills and talents when they later resume employment. We know that this pattern imposes large and long-term losses on women, and we would be surprised if it did not entail large and long-term losses for employers and the economy. The costs of inadequate childcare provision would need to be calculated, as well as the costs and gains of developing good quality services based on workers receiving pay and conditions appropriate to their work. Proper comparisons would also need to take into account not only what the total costs were, but also how these costs were distributed – who carried the costs, both now and in a proposed alternative approach.

There are many doubts and uncertainties about how best to proceed, born of decades of neglect. While other countries have slowly begun to try to connect the world of employment and the world of parenthood, Britain has ignored the matter, remaining wedded to an outdated view about parenthood and childcare. The time for a change is long overdue.

APPENDIX I

Tables

Abbreviations

Last occupation before birth of child	P,M	– Professional and managerial
	OO	– Other occupations, e.g. secretarial, clerical, sales, manual.
Type of childcare	N	– Nursery
	CM	– Childminder or shared nanny
	R	– Relative
	O	– Other

INTRODUCTION

Table 0.1 *Employment status and childcare arrangements of women in the sample when they first resumed work and at second interview when the child was 10 to 11 months old*

	Last occupation before birth of child		Not employed	Employed: Childcare arrangement N	CM	R	O
First resumed work	P,M (N=139)	%	14*	21	46	14	4
	OO (N=116)	%	29*	3	26	35	6
	Total (N=255)	%	21*	13	37	24	5
At second interview	P,M (N=136)	%	21	22	42	10	4
	OO (N=110)	%	37	4	27	26	7
	Total (N=246)	%	28	14	36	17	4

* Includes all women who did not resume work at any time up to second interview.

NB: Five of the employed women resumed work in a part-time job: by the second interview, 12 women had part-time jobs.

CHAPTER 1 – Putting it in context

Table 1.1 *Places in publicly-funded childcare* for children under three years per 100 children under three in various European countries (mid 1980s)*

Country	%	Country	%	Country	%
Belgium	17%	Greece	3%	Portugal	4%
Denmark	44%†	Italy	5%	Sweden	30%†
France	24%	Luxembourg	1%	UK	2%
Germany	2%	Netherlands	1%		

* Includes publicly-funded day nurseries, nursery education and childminders.

† Figures for children using services, not places in services. The figure for places will be lower because some children (less than a third) attend part-time.

Source: EEC Childcare Network; Leira (1987).

Table 1.2 *Proportion (%) of women with children under five years who are employed and in the labour force in various countries*

	Not in labour force	Unemployed	Employed (a): hours per week			Total employed
			1–19	20–29	30+	
Belgium 1985	31	17	6	10	36	52
Denmark 1985	16	12	4	16	53	73
France 1985	41	9	4	6	36	50
Germany 1985	61	7	—	—	—	32
Greece 1985	60	5	1	5	28	35
Italy 1985	57	5	3	5	30	38
Luxembourg 1985	65	3	3	7	23	33
Netherlands 1985	75	4	11	5	4	21
Norway 1983	46	—	—	—	—	54*
Ireland 1985	74	7	2	3	12	19
Sweden 1983	18	—	—	—	—	82†
UK 1985	61	11	15	5	9	29
Canada 1984	48	8	—	—	—	44*
USA 1986	46	6	—	—	—	48‡
Australia 1986	59	4	24		13	37

* Proportion of women with children under three
† Proportion of women with children under seven
‡ Proportion of women with children under six
(a): In most countries there are some employed women for whom there is no information on hours of employment. The numbers are small except in the case of France, where this group accounts for 4% of all women.

Source: 1985 Labour Force Survey; Leira (1987); US Department of Labour, private communication; Statistics Canada, 'The Labour Force' (Ottawa, December 1984); Australian Bureau of Statistics (1986).

CHAPTER 2 Deciding to go back to work

Table 2.1 *Women's main reasons for resuming work, at first interview*

Main reason for resuming work	*Last occupation before birth of child* P,M (N=101)	OO (N=80)	Total (N=181)
	%	%	%
Money	21	40	30
Housing	23	33	28
Job and Home factors	22	9	15
Other	20	9	15
More than one given	14	9	11

Table 2.2 *Whose earnings contribute to items of household expenditure at second interview (N=170)*

Items of expenditure		*Wife's earnings*	*Joint/ variable*	*Husband's earnings*
Childcare	%	49	34	17
Child's daily needs	%	35	51	14
Daily household items	%	31	46	23
Child's other items	%	27	59	14
Housing	%	21	45	34
Phone	%	21	54	25
Fuel	%	20	52	26
Car	%	12	61	27

Table 2.3 *When women made their decisions to resume employment (N=188)*

Before pregnancy	61%
During pregnancy	18%
First three months after birth	14%
Second three months after birth	8%

CHAPTER 3 – On maternity leave: thinking about the return

Table 3.1 *Dissatisfaction with motherhood and being at home before return at first interview*

Note on methodology: Women were rated on a four-point Dissatisfaction Scale (none; low; moderate; high) on the basis of their replies to a range of questions on motherhood and being at home. There was a high degree of agreement between the two people who independently rated the levels of dissatisfaction.

Employment Intentions at first interview	Last occupation before birth		Dissatisfaction None/low	Moderate	High
To resume work	P,M (N=100)	%	47	38	15
	OO (N=77)	%	43	35	22
	Total (N=177)	%	45	37	18
Not to resume work	P,M (N=27)	%	67	26	7
	OO (N=39)	%	79	18	5
	Total (N=66)	%	73	21	6

Table 3.2 *Doubts and anxieties before resuming work, at first interview*

Last occupation before birth		*No doubts felt*	*Occasional doubts*	*A lot of doubts*	*Other*
P,M (N=102)	%	31	41	27	1
OO (N=81)	%	33	42	24	1
Total (N=183)	%	32	42	25	1

Table 3.3 *Women's attitudes to mothers of young children working full-time 'from choice rather than necessity', at first interview*

Employment intentions at first interview	*Last occupation before birth*		*Not right*	*Undecided*	*Right*
To resume work	P,M (N=104)	%	12	3	85
	OO (N=78)	%	26	6	68
	Total (N=182)	%	18	4	77
Not to resume work	P,M (N=27)	%	48	4	48
	OO (N=39)	%	67	8	26
	Total (N=66)	%	59	6	35

Table 3.4 *Feelings of obligation to return or not to return to work, at first interview*

Employment intentions at first interview	*Last occupation before birth*		*Felt no obligation*	*Felt obligation both to return* and *not to return*	*Felt obligation not to return*	*Felt obligation to return*
To resume work	P,M (N=104)	%	19	22	3	56
	OO (N=79)	%	27	24	5	44
	Total (N=183)	%	23	23	4	50
Not to resume work	P,M (N=27)	%	37	15	37	11
	OO (N=40)	%	47	15	30	8
	Total (N=67)	%	43	15	33	9

Table 3.5 *Felt choice about return to work, at first interview*

Employment intention at first interview	*Last occupation before birth*		*Felt had:* No choice	Choice	Don't know
To resume work	P,M (N=104)	%	37	61	2
	OO (N=81)	%	43	57	—
	Total (N=185)	%	40	59	1
Not to resume work	P,M (N=28)	%	7	93	
	OO (N=40)	%	23	77	
	Total (N=68)	%	16	84	

Table 3.6 *Feelings of obligation to child to return to work, at first interview*

Employment intentions at first interview	*Last occupation before birth*		*Felt no obligation*	*Felt obligation both to return* and *not to return*	*Felt obligation not to return*	*Felt obligation to return*
To resume work	P,M (N=104)	%	73	1	21	5
	OO (N=79)	%	68	6	23	3
	Total (N=183)	%	71	3	22	4
Not to resume work	P,M (N=27	%	48	—	52	—
	OO (N=39)	%	54	—	46	—
	Total (N=66)	%	52	—	49	—

Table 3.7 *Feelings of obligation to self to return to work, at first interview*

Employment intentions at first interview	*Last occupation before birth*		*Felt no obligation*	*Felt obligation both to return* and *not to return*	*Felt obligation not to return*	*Felt obligation to return*
To resume work	P,M (N=104)	%	43	—	1	55
	OO (N=79)	%	62	—	—	38
	Total (N=183)	%	52	—	—	48
Not to resume work	P,M (N=27)	%	82	—	7	11
	OO (N=39)	%	87	—	8	5
	Total (N=66)	%	84	—	8	8

Table 3.8 *Women's employment preferences, at first interview (i.e. before most women had resumed employment)*

Employment intentions at first interview	*Last occupation before birth of child*		*Employment preference:*			
			Not to resume work	*To resume part-time*	*To resume full-time*	*Other/ Don't know*
To resume work	P,M (N=104)	%	13	55	27	5
	OO (N=81)	%	22	58	15	5
	Total (N=185)	%	17	56	22	5
Not to resume work	P,M (N=29)	%	76	21	—	3
	OO (N=40)	%	55	43	—	2
	Total (N=69)	%	64	33	—	3

CHAPTER 4 – Finding childcare

Table 4.1 *Ideal childcare arrangements compared to childcare found and used*

Type of childcare found/used		*'Ideal' childcare:* N	*CM*	*R*	*Nanny*	*Other*
N – Found* (N=38)	%	77	9	—	14	—
Used* (N=30)	%	77	3	—	13	7
CM – Found (N=77)	%	23	37	11	25	5
Used (N=78)	%	15	65	4	12	5
R – Found (N=51)	%	15	5	67	11	2
Used (N=35)	%	14	3	71	6	6
Total – Found	%	32	21	26	18	3
Used	%	27	35	19	11	9

* '*Found*' refers to childcare arrangements made at first interview, before the mother resumed employment.

'*Used*' refers to childcare arrangements used at second interview when the child was 10 to 11 months old.

CHAPTER 5 – Back to work

Table 5.1 *Provisions made by employers for working parents and/or that women mention ought to be made by employers, for women employed at second interview (N=170).*

	Provided by employer	*Ought to be provided*
Flexible or part-time hours	5%	18%
Childcare	18%	56%
Time off if child ill etc.	9%	31%
Other	5%	16%

Table 5.2 *Attitude of bosses and colleagues on return to work for women employed at second interview*

	Last occupation before birth		*Attitude to women on return:* Positive	Indifferent	Mixed/ wholly negative
Bosses	P,M (N=102)	%	46	29	25
	OO (N=70)	%	50	33	17
	Total (N=172)	%	48	31	21
Colleagues	P,M (N=101)	%	30	7	63
	OO (N=68)	%	33	18	49
	Total (N=169)	%	31	11	57

CHAPTER 6 – How childcare worked out

Table 6.1 *Satisfaction with childcare arrangements on 12-item checklist, at second interview*

Checklist item	*Level of satisfaction*		*Type of childcare used:* N (*n*=31)	CM (N=79)	R (N=34)	*Total* (N=151)
Cost	S*	%	41	66	80	64
	D*	%	15	6	4	7
Distance, time and effort to get there	S	%	48	61	58	58
	D	%	29	6	13	13
Personality or motivation of caregivers	S	%	64	78	91	78
	D	%	7	4	—	4
Your child's sleeping, feeding, or toilet training	S	%	42	61	82	62
	D	%	7	4	3	8
How your child spends his/her day/ the stimulation he/she gets	S	%	65	72	77	71
	D	%	—	3	—	1
Diet, safety, cleanliness, physical care	S	%	48	75	88	72
	D	%	3	5	3	5
Affection and warmth shown to child by caretakers	S	%	81	89	94	88
	D	%	3	4	—	3

The number of other children at caretakers	S	%	29	66	72	60
	D	%	13	5	3	6
Discipline and management of your child's behaviour	S	%	48	72	62	65
	D	%	10	—	—	2
Age, experience, qualifications, ability of caretakers	S	%	55	75	88	74
	D	%	3	1	—	2
Hours that arrangement available	S	%	52	78	97	78
	D	%	16	4	—	5
Standard of accommodation and/or facilities (e.g. toys, outdoor space)	S	%	64	78	91	78
	D	%	7	4	—	4

* S = % who rated item 'very satisfied'
D = % who rated item 'a bit dissatisfied' or 'very dissatisfied'
Two other options were available for each item – 'quite satisfied' and 'neither satisfied nor dissatisfied'.

Table 6.2 *Mothers who would like to talk more with child's caregiver or have disagreed with her, at second interview*

		Type of childcare used: N (N=30)	CM (N=81)	R (N=36)	*Total* (N=147)
Would like to talk more with caregiver in general	%	41	25	11	24
Have specific subject would like to talk more about	%	30	22	17	20
Had difference of opinion with caregiver	%	33	32	39	32
Disagreed with caregiver, but not said anything	%	63	33	22	37

Table 6.3 *Childcare placements that end in a move or produce childcare difficulties, up to second interview*

	Placement in: N (N=36)	CM (N=114)	R (N=70)	*Total* (N=240)
	%	%	%	%
Childcare placements that ended in move				
– because child's family moved	—	3	—	1
– to or from temporary placement	—	4	19	8
– because of problem with childcare	3	15	10	11
Childcare difficulty	—	5	4	5

CHAPTER 7 – What it feels like

Table 7.1 *Feelings of women who resume work on leaving their children at caregivers*

		Feelings on leaving child: Mostly or wholly negative	Acceptance or acceptance with occasional negative	Mainly/wholly positive
When first left child (N=171)	%	74	19	7
On leaving child at second interview (N=165)	%	11	75	14

Table 7.2 *Negative feelings of mothers who return to work (N=171)*

		Never felt	*Did feel: no longer*	*Still feels on occasions*	*Feels often*
Guilt	%	37	21	31	11
Jealousy of caregiver	%	68	10	18	4
Rejected by child	%	82	3	14	1

Table 7.3 *Change in tiredness between first and second interview (i.e. between when the child was 4 to 5 months old and 10 to 11 months old)*

Note on methodology: Women were rated on a four-point scale of tiredness, on the basis of their replies to questioning about the extent and nature of their tiredness.

		Tiredness rating between first and second interview: Increased	Stayed the same	Reduced
Employed full-time (N=171)	%	34	47	19
Not employed (N=58)	%	12	55	33

Table 7.4 *How women feel about their decision to return or not to return to work, at second interview*

Employment status	*Last occupation before birth*		*Feelings about decision:* Wholly/mainly positive	*Very mixed*	*Wholly/mainly negative*
Employed	P,M (N=102)	%	82	5	13
	OO (N=69)	%	77	7	15
	Total (N=171)	%	80	6	14
Not employed	P,M (N=26)	%	77	12	11
	OO (N=32)	%	84	13	3
	Total (N=58)	%	81	12	7

CHAPTER 8 – How women cope

Table 8.1 *If women who have resumed work feel they are coping as well as they would like, at second interview*

Last occupation before birth		*Coping as well as would like*	*Not coping as well as would like*	*Don't know*
P,M (N=98)	%	56	43	1
OO (N=67)	%	73	27	—
Total (N=165)	%	63	37	1

Table 8.2 *How women who have resumed work describe themselves as coping, at second interview*

Last occupation before birth		*Describes self as:* Coping badly	*Coping well in some ways, badly in others*	*Coping quite well*	*Coping very well*
P,M (N=101)	%	4	11	53	32
OO (N=67)	%	3	6	36	55
Total (N=165)	%	4	9	46	41

Table 8.3 *Housework management strategies adopted by women who resume work, at second interview (N=168)*

Housework management strategies		*Applies to women:* Not at all	*To some extent*	*To a great extent*
Try to plan ahead	%	10	55	35
Plan/use time economically	%	21	54	26
Reduce jobs in the home	%	21	58	21
Lower standards	%	26	59	15
Work harder in the home	%	40	42	19
Keep to a strict routine	%	65	25	10

Table 8.4 *Positive attitudes adopted by women who have resumed work, at second interview (N=168)*

Positive attitudes adopted		*Applies to women:* Not at all	*To some extent*	*To a great extent*
I think it's all worthwhile in the long run	%	2	38	60
I tend to look on the bright side	%	6	56	38
I try not to dwell on the difficult side of things	%	15	55	30
I feel like giving up because it's all too much	%	84	14	2
I tend to dwell on the difficult side of life	%	63	33	3

Note on methodology for Tables 8.3, 8.4: Women were asked to complete two questionnaires which covered ways in which working mothers may cope at a practical level and 'ways in which people think about themselves'. For each item, women were asked to choose one of three options which best described them: 'applies not at all', 'applies to some extent' and 'applies to a great extent'.

CHAPTER 9 – Husbands and fathers

Note on methodology for Table 9.1: Women were asked to complete questionnaires showing what proportion of childcare tasks and housework tasks they normally did. For *childcare* there were five items – bathing/washing; dressing; seeing to child in evening or night; feeding; changing nappies. For *housework* there were seven items – preparing main meals; shopping; clearing up after meals; washing clothes; ironing; hoovering; cleaning. For each item, there were five options – do 'none of it', (score 0); do 'some of it – less than half' (score 1); do 'about half' (score 2); do 'most of it' (score 3); do 'all of it' (score 4). These scores were then added to produce a 'total childcare' and 'total housework score' for women. The 'total childcare score' ranges from 0 (i.e. does no items ever) to 20 (does all of all items); the 'total housework score' ranges from 0 (i.e. does no items ever) to 28 (does all of all items).

Table 9.1 *Total childcare and housework scores for women in full-time employment at second interview*

		Score:						*Average Score (Mean)*
		0–8	*9–12*	*13–16*	*17–20*	*21–24*	*25–28*	
Total childcare score (N=150)	%	6	37	37	20	—	—	13.4
Total housework score (N=156)	%	1	8	17	31	24	19	19.5

Table 9.2 *The frequency with which fathers married to women employed full-time do childcare and housework tasks at second interview*

		Never/in emergency	*Sometimes*	*At least once a week but less than 4x a week*	*Most days*	*Every day*
Childcare tasks (N=172)						
Changing nappies	%	13	12	30	24	22
Feeding	%	8	14	35	26	17
Bathing/washing	%	17	24	28	22	8
Dressing	%	8	17	40	20	14
Playing	%	1	1	5	37	57
Housework tasks (N=172)						
Prepare main meals	%	21	25	30	17	8
Clearing up meals	%	11	15	24	35	15
Shopping	%	18	24		58	
Hoovering	%	26	33		41	
Other cleaning	%	35	32		33	
Washing clothes	%	64	17		20	
Ironing	%	66	17		18	

APPENDIX II

Different types of leave to assist working parents

1 Statutory Maternity Leave in the UK

The legislation enacted in 1975 and implemented in 1976 provided women with a right to stop work 11 weeks before the birth of a baby and to return to existing employment up to 29 weeks following confinement. To be eligible, an employee had to have been continuously employed *with the same employer* for at least two years before the beginning of the 11th week prior to the expected date of confinement, if she normally worked for 16 or more hours a week. If she normally worked between eight and 16 hours, then she had to have been continuously employed with the same employer for five years.

Since then, a number of further conditions have been added:

1 In 1980, employers of fewer than five workers were exempted from reinstating women when 'not reasonably practicable'.
2 Reinstatement procedures were made more complicated, so that to maintain her entitlement, a woman may have to provide her employer with three written notifications of her intention to return to work, and with a certificate of the expected date of confinement, all at specified times.
3 Since 1980, reinstatement in 'existing employment' has meant not necessarily the same job, but one that in terms and conditions is not less favourable.

2 Statutory Maternity Pay in the UK

Before April 1987, women might qualify for Maternity Allowance, paid under the National Insurance scheme by the DHSS, and Maternity Pay paid under the Employment Protection Act by the Department of Employment. Since April 6 1987, these two benefits have been merged to form Statutory Maternity Pay (SMP). SMP is paid at two rates.

1. *Higher rate SMP* is paid at 90 per cent of normal earnings. It is payable for the first six weeks of absence to women who work 16 hours or more a week and have worked for the same employer for at least two years. Women who work eight to 16 hours a week qualify if they have worked for the same employer for at least five years.
2. *Lower rate SMP* is paid at a flat rate, equal to the lower rate of Statutory Sick Pay (£32.85 from 6 April 1987). It is paid for a further 12 weeks to women who have received the higher rate for six weeks. Women who do not qualify for the higher rate, but who nevertheless have worked for the same employer for at least six months, will qualify for the lower rate for the full 18 weeks maternity pay period.

Other features of the scheme are:

1. To qualify, women must have had average earnings above the Lower Earnings Limit for National Insurance Contributions (currently £38) for at least eight weeks.
2. The employment and earnings test for the above (1) will be applied at the end of the 15th week before the baby is due.
3. SMP will be taxable and subject to national insurance contributions.
4. SMP will be paid for a 'core period' of 13 weeks starting six weeks before the baby is due. The other five weeks can be chosen by the woman.

3 Statutory Maternity Leave and Pay in other countries

All European countries have maternity leave legislation. Compared to the United Kingdom, the period of post-natal leave in Western Europe is generally shorter, varying from 6 weeks in the Netherlands to 14 weeks in Denmark. In Scandinavia, there has been a trend to convert part of maternity leave to parental leave, which can be taken by either parent (parental leave is discussed further below). In Finland, for instance, maternity leave (before and after birth) used to be 258 days; since 1985, however, the last 158 days may be taken by either parent. This development has gone furthest in Sweden, where there is now no maternity leave as such: all 52 weeks of post-natal leave is equally available to mothers and fathers.

Unlike the UK, other European countries provide benefit payment for the full period of the leave. In all cases these benefits are earnings-related throughout, ranging from 70% of earnings in Ireland to 100% in Greece, Germany and several other countries. The UK is also unusual in its qualifying conditions, which are the most stringent in Europe. These conditions involve a 'continuous employment requirement', that is the woman concerned should have worked continuously *for the same employer* for a period of time. In other countries, qualifying conditions are limited to a period of time in the general workforce and/or a certain level of social security contributions. To qualify in Italy, for instance, a woman must be employed and insured at the beginning of pregnancy, while in Denmark the claimant must be insured and working for six months during one year preceding confinement, including at least 40 hours in the four weeks preceding leave.

Maternity leave legislation is also widely available outside Europe, including many Third World countries. To take two examples, in Saudi Arabia employers allow women four weeks off before the birth and six weeks after, together with between 50 to 100 per cent of earnings. In Mongolia women are paid in full by the state for 45 days prior to birth and for 56 days after birth.

Two major exceptions to the provision of statutory maternity leave are Australia and the United States. In Australia, most women can get maternity leave, but under the terms of industrial awards rather than legislation. The qualifying condition is, like the UK, a continuous employment requirement, usually 12 months with the same employer. The total period of maternity leave in most awards is 52 weeks, usually unpaid. Paid leave (up to a maximum of 12 weeks) is only available in the public service. In the United States there is no national law entitling women to maternity leave. Paid maternity leave is available to about 40% of women, in most cases only for 6 to 8 weeks. Where provided, it is usually part of the benefits provided by employers for their workforce, and as such is still largely available only to women who work in large organisations. Some employers also permit their female employees brief additional unpaid but job protected leaves. Finally, five states provide disability benefit, at a modest level, for women away from work at the time of maternity.

4. Paternity leave

This is a period of leave given to men at the time of the birth of their child and is not to be confused with parental leave. It enables fathers to be present at the birth and to be with their partner and new child for a short period after the birth. It coincides with maternity leave, although it is of much shorter duration, lasting at most for a couple of weeks. There is no statutory paternity leave in the UK, nor in most other European countries. A notable exception is Sweden, which allows fathers ten days leave at the birth of a child.

5 Parental leave

Parental leave enables parents (fathers as well as mothers) to stay at home to take sole or principal charge of the child following the end of maternity leave. In a two parent family it is taken by one parent at a time and is not normally allowed unless both parents are in employment. Parental leave is becoming widely available in Europe. It has been implemented, or is about to be implemented, by all countries in Scandinavia and in the E.E.C. except Ireland and the UK. The UK has opposed an E.E.C. draft directive which proposes to introduce a minimum standard for parental leave throughout the Community. The proposal includes three months of parental leave per parent per child, to be taken at any time between the end of maternity leave and the child's second birthday; the draft Directive also proposes that the leave could be taken part-time, and its length extended proportionately, if the employer agrees.

Existing parental leave schemes vary considerably. In Denmark, for instance, the last ten weeks of the 24 weeks of post-natal leave can be taken by either parent. In Greece each parent is entitled to take three months unpaid leave before the child is two and a half. In Norway, parents are entitled to unpaid leave for up to 3 years, to be taken before their child's tenth birthday.

Most statutory parental leave is unpaid or paid at a low flat rate. Some countries allow parents taking leave the option of working part time. In Sweden parents of pre-school children are entitled to extensive parental leave, nine months of which is fully paid and three months at a low flat rate. Parents can take the leave on a part or full-time basis. They are also entitled to work a six hour working day (until their child is seven years of age) but without any compensation for loss of earnings.

6 Time off to breastfeed

Once back at work some countries allow mothers time off to breastfeed their children. In Portugal, for instance, women are allowed one hour off in the day until the child is a year old.

7 Leave for family reasons

This is a period of leave which enables an employee with 'family responsibilities' to undertake pressing family duties, such as the care of a sick child or partner, or taking a child to the doctor. Working parents in Sweden are allowed up to 60 days of paid leave a year for the care of a sick child up to twelve years old. They are also allowed two special days off every year to visit a childcare centre or school or to settle their children into school or daycare. Such provision is also available in a few other countries though the amount is less generous.

SOME USEFUL ORGANISATIONS

The Equal Opportunities Commission, Overseas House, Quay Street, Manchester M3 3HN. Tel: 061 837 9244.

Established by Parliament in 1975, to eliminate sex discrimination and generally encourage equal opportunities for men and women. Can provide advice and guidance on specific problems concerning maternity leave and discrimination.

Maternity Alliance, 15 Britannia Street, London WC1X 9JP. Tel: 01 837 1261.

A national organisation which campaigns for improvements in rights and services for mothers, fathers and babies. It works for better provision before conception, and during pregnancy, childbirth and the first year of life.

Publications include:
Maternity Action, the bulletin of the Alliance, published five times a year. Free to members: otherwise £6 a year.
Working Parents Rights, a Maternity Alliance Charter (1987). Cost £2.50.
Maternity Rights Handbook – Know Your Rights (1984). Written by Ruth Evans and Lyn Durward and published by Penguin Books. Cost £4.95.

National Childbirth Trust, 9 Queensborough Terrace, London W2 7TB. Tel: 01 221 3833

A national organisation concerned with education for pregnancy, birth and parenthood with over 300 branches and groups throughout the UK. Organises antenatal classes and a system of postnatal support for new mothers. Some branches have working mothers groups and/or nanny share registers.

National Childminding Association. 8 Masons Hill, Bromley, Kent BR2 9SY. Tel: 01 464 6164

A national organisation, with local branches, organised to support and advise anyone concerned with childminding, including parents and local authority workers as well as childminders themselves.

Publications include:
An information pack, which includes a brief guide for parents – '*So you want to find a childminder*'. Send SAE.
'*I need a childminder*', a longer guide to parents considering childminding. Cost 50p.

Working Mothers Association, 23 Webbs Road, London SW11 6RU. Tel: 01 228 3757

A national organisation offering information on childcare options, and support to working mothers through some 90 local groups.

Publications include:
Working Mothers Association Newsletter, published four times a year, free to members.
The Working Mothers Handbook – a Practical Guide to the Alternatives in Childcare. Cost £2.

Workplace Nurseries Campaign, Room 205, Southbank House, Black Prince Road, London SE1 7SJ. Tel: 01 582 7199

A national organisation which provides information and advice on setting up workplace nurseries and other forms of workplace childcare. Includes a consultancy service.

Publications include:
An information pack on how to set up a workplace nursery.

BIBLIOGRAPHY

Arber, S., Gilbert, N., and Dale, A. (1985) 'Paid employment and women's health: a benefit or a source of role strain' *Sociology of Health and Illness*, *7, No 3*

Bell, C., McKee, L. and Priestley, K. (1983) *Fathers, Childbirth and Work* Equal Opportunities Commission: Manchester

Brannen, J. (1987) 'Taking maternity leave: the employment decisions of women with young children' *TCRU Occasional Paper No 7* Thomas Coram Research Unit: London

Brannen, J. and Moss, P. (1987a) 'Women's financial contributions in dual-earner households after the birth of the first child' in Brannen, J. and Wilson, G. (Eds) *Give and take in families: studies in resource distribution* Allen and Unwin: London

Brown, C. (1984) *Black and White in Britain* Heinemann: London

Brown, G. and Harris, T. (1978) *The Social Origins of Depression* Tavistock: London

Daniel, W. (1980) *Maternity Rights: The Experience of Women* PSI: London

Dex, S. (1983) *The Sexual Division of Work: Conceptual Revolutions in the Social Sciences* Harvester Press: Brighton

Graham, H. (1982) 'Coping or How Women are Seen and Not Heard' in Friedman, S. and Sarah, E. (Eds) *On the Problems of Women* Women's Press: London

Joshi, H. (1987) 'The Cost of Caring' in Millar, J. and Glendinning, C. (Eds) *Women and Poverty* Wheatsheaf: Brighton

Leira, A. (1987) *Day Care for Children in Denmark, Norway and Sweden* Institute for Social Research: Oslo

Lewis, C. and O'Brien, M. (Eds) (1987) *Reassessing Fatherhood: New Observations on Fathers and the Modern Family* Sage Publications: London

Martin, J. and Roberts, C. (1984) *Women and Employment: A Lifetime Perspective* HMSO: London

Mayall, B. and Petrie, P. (1983) *Childminding and Day Nurseries – What Kind of Care?* Heinemann: London

McKee, L. and O'Brien, M. (Eds) (1982) *The Father Figure* Tavistock: London
Moss, P. (1986) 'Child Care in the Early Months: How Child Care Arrangements are made for Babies.' *TCRU Occasional Paper No 3* Thomas Coram Research Unit: London
Moss, P. (1987) 'A Review of Childminding Research' *TCRU Occasional Paper No 6* Thomas Coram Research Unit: London
New, C. and David, M. (1985) *For the Children's Sake* Penguin: London
Oakley, A. (1974a) *Housewife* Allen Lane: London
Oakley, A. (1974b) *The Sociology of Housework* Martin Robertson: Oxford
Oakley, A. (1979) *From Here to Maternity: Becoming a Mother* Penguin Books: Harmondsworth
Oakley, A. (1980) *Women Confined: Towards a Sociology of Childbirth* Martin Robertson: Oxford
Pearlin, L. and Schooler, C. (1978) 'The Structure of Coping' *Journal of Health and Social Behaviour, 19*
Roll, J. (1986) *Babies and Money: birth trends and costs* Family Policy Studies Centre: London
Russell, G. (1983) *The Changing Role of Fathers* Open University Press: Milton Keynes
Scarr, S. and Dunn, J. (1987) *Mother Care, Other Care* Penguin Books: Harmondsworth
Sharpe, S. (1984) *Double Identity: the lives of working mothers* Penguin Books: Harmondsworth
Tizard, B. (1986) 'The Care of Young Children: Implications of Recent Research' *TCRU Occasional Paper No 1* Thomas Coram Research Unit: London
Urwin, C. (1985) 'Constructing motherhood: the persuasion of normal development' in C. Steadman, C. Urwin and V. Walkerdine (Eds) *Language, Gender and Childhood* Routledge and Kegan Paul: London
Warr, P. and Parry, G. (1981) *Paid Employment and Women's Psychological Well-being* Social and Applied Psychology Unit Paper
Zambrana, R., Hurst, M., and Hite, R. (1979) 'The Working Mother in Contemporary Perspectives: a Review of the Literature' *Paediatrics*, 64

INDEX